Sailing From Behind the Curve

DAVE BACON

Judy,

Thanks for all your help. It has made a difference.

Dave Bacon

DEDICATION

This book is foremost dedicated to my younger brother, Bob Bacon who wanted to know this story. Without his curiosity and questioning this book never would have been written.

If you've ever owned or sailed on a Bear, this book is also dedicated to you.

ACKNOWLEDGEMENT

Publishing a book is a joint project requiring the help and cooperation of others. The people involved bring special skills, whether it be editing, proof reading, art, or formatting the book into a final product.

Richard Herman, as editor, was of considerable assistance when it came to guiding the events of this true account. Judy Person, as proof reader, saw to the punctuation and grammatical aspects with excellent results.

Gretchen Ricker did a great job formatting the book. Russell and Christine Katz provided the early history of Renegade, Bear number 35, and additional information regarding the Bear Class.

There are others who gave their direct support to making the cruise a reality. Susan Damon, my former wife handled all of my mail and personal finances. Tony Gaetani, invested his time and resources to make the Bear ready. Without their dedicated help the cruise may never have taken place.

For all of you who played a part in this cruise and anyone I may have forgotten, thank you!

CONTENTS

Images

A FOREWORD

In his first book, *The Gentle Art of Pottering*, Dave Bacon carved out a special niche in the sailing world and created a mini-masterpiece on messing about in small sailboats. His boat of choice was the West Wight Potter 15, a small micro cruiser that can, in the hands of a master sailor, do amazing things.

And Dave Bacon is that skipper.

But how he matured into a master mariner is a story in itself, and, although he would cringe at that label, he looked into his past and with the perspective that only passing years can bring, takes the reader on that voyage in *Sailing From Behind the Curve*.

That story starts in a Junior High School where Dave had been teaching for 10 years. He was a good teacher and liked working with twelve and thirteen-year-olds. But they are a tough age group and he was experiencing the onset of burnout. He needed to hit the reset button and turned to his first love, sailing small boats.

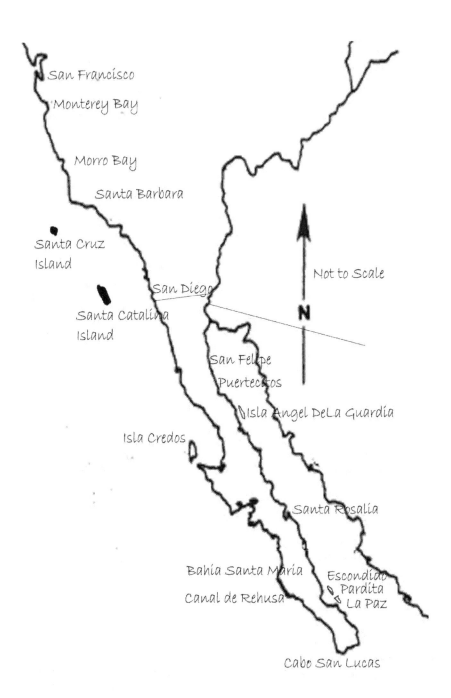

1 BOUND TO SEA

All the other boats had turned back. Their skippers had seen the incoming fog and felt the weight of its increasing wind. Bound to sea and searching for answers, turning back was not an option.

The dull grey Pacific swells continued to steepen obscuring the Point Pinos light except when Ah Tiller the Fun, my Potter 15 sloop, topped the crests. Sailing on through the fog, any connection with the coast was soon lost. From my position on the rail I watched the compass, both feet tucked under the hiking strap, moving with the unpredictable motion of the boat much as an experienced horseman would when riding. Sailing confidently ahead of the curve, I was determined to cross my old outbound track.

It had been 34 years since I was outbound to Mexico for a cruise to the Sea of Cortez. But as I reminisce about it now, I still shudder to think about the possibilities of what could have happened when sailing so far behind the curve as I did back then. However, off I went, full of confidence into the adventure of a lifetime. I suppose that many people would wonder why someone such as me, or others, would want to drop everything, leaving their jobs, and take on such a challenge.

"Because it's there" is not a real answer. An honest answer would have a deeper meaning and greater sense of purpose. Maybe some people might be attracted to such a quest just for the adventure of it, or temporarily driven to it as an effort to escape a dreary life, perhaps even one with a dark side. We may never know a person's real reasons for taking on such a challenge.

As for me, I had my reasons just like anyone else.

Life ashore is quite different from that at sea. Ashore, when you're in trouble there's a social support system to set you on the right path as you come to terms with the consequences of your actions. But at sea it's different. Violate these laws and your fate is determined by an impersonal jury of wind and wave. Seamanship is always your best defense in this case, but the only appeal you'll ever get is luck. Without that, wrecking the boat on some foreign shore or just failing to ever show up again will be the final consequence of all your efforts. Of course it's best to know this before you start out. And I thought I knew it at the time, but not the cold hard reality of it. The only way to understand that is to sail through the worst of it.

Having crossed my outbound track, the cold spray that penetrated the neck of my parka instantly brought me back to the present. The predictable conditions that I had so confidently sailed in a short while ago had vanished. Now finding myself behind the curve, quick action was demanded if I were to survive. The trick was to turn the boat quickly through the steepening waves to avoid being capsized. With my retreat back to the harbor seriously threatened, it all came down to just a matter of waiting for the exact instant to turn the boat. Once the sheets were clear and free to run, the moment was chosen. Ah Tiller the Fun spun off the wind, surfing the face of the first wave to overtake it as the mainsheet continued to run out to the knot.

"Watch it," I said to myself, quickly countering a dangerous roll as the boom arced skyward and the Potter surfed hard. The little boat, moving too fast for safety, demanded my very best on the face of each wave as the crests continued to pass under.

Once back in the bay, the little sloop was safely jibed over. With the jib winged out, a course was set toward the harbor. The relaxing warmth of the sun felt good and the tension began to ebb away, giving me time to think about what had just happened.

What was this destructive behavior that drove me to sail this way? A capsize would have been fatal. Certainly there were hidden issues deep inside that needed to be uncovered. I had come to realize that the only way to successfully face them was head on. And the best way would be to write the Sea of Cortez story. For me, this meant entering the cave of the dragon, pulling him into the full light of day, and finding the answers necessary to sort out the conflicting emotions I continued to harbor regarding my actions during the cruise.

Exhilarated after such a challenging sail and now fully understanding what must be done, my course was set.

Elated, "Cheated Death Again", often chanted by the 'Usual Suspects' at the end of a cruise sprang to mind.

Or in this instance, for me, being bold enough to start the search for answers to my troubling conflict, that I had avoided for so very long.

2 EARLY BEGINNINGS

Was I taking on more than I could handle? That was a question I had yet to answer. Meanwhile, the assistant superintendent droned on in his dreary little office about my contractual obligations. Doubt and fear like an unwanted fog continued to creep over the proceedings. For the first time in my life, I was really on my own and not sheltered by someone else's care or authority. I was deeply driven by the thought that my life needed real change. One way or another, change was coming. With the contract already set before me, I was offered a pen.

"Well, this is it," I thought. "Either sign it or resign from teaching." Driven by the need for change, but ruled by a desire for security, I put pen to paper and did my duty. But by taking the easy way out, opting for a sabbatical for the 1981-82 school year, I had unknowingly changed the whole course of my life.

The contract had been signed to gain time. I had problems and needed to deal with them. Not only was school going badly, but my fourteen-year marriage was also failing. It was my fault.

I'm sure that the depression I was suffering had something to do with it. Dark depression, the kind where I saw no alternative but to retreat into my myself and hide from any interaction as my mind rambled on and on about all the bad things that had ever happened, and how powerless I was to control them. It was a darkness that overshadowed everything, the kind that drew me in without choice, then robbed me of the life I once knew.

In complete desperation, I grabbed at any meaningful thing left. And it was from within that immobilizing darkness that I desperately grabbed onto sailing, the thing I knew best, and began the slow difficult voyage back into the happier life I once knew.

It had been nine years since I began teaching middle school, and like many others in the field, I was reaching the end of my rope. The idea of facing another school year at this point was quite impossible to contemplate. The sabbatical was my logical last grasp at the proverbial straw. With the coming school year, I'd be placed on half pay while I did a travel study in Mexico. All I had to do was to produce a curriculum that could be used in the classroom. Little did I know at the time of signing, just how much pressure I was placing on myself. If I failed to produce a curriculum or didn't come back for the following year, the money I had been paid, half my annual salary, would have to be paid back.

On the other hand, it was a nice idea to use Dancing Bear, my twenty-three-foot Bear class sloop, to travel from port to port learning about the Mexican culture. It was certainly a much nicer idea than the dreariness of correcting endless piles of student's papers. But as they say, in for a penny, in for a pound.

The days began to fly by. The darkness and depression I was feeling slowly decreased as I excitedly planned for the cruise. It was good to have goals again. It helped me feel in charge, much better than stumbling through the constant challenge of teaching.

All manner of things were needed for this cruise. There were charts, light lists, and cruising guides, just to name a few. Organizing my own home study course, I learned how to navigate using both coastal and celestial methods. Many problems came up during the early stages of planning that required answers. What will I need, and how can I stow everything in such a small boat?

Fortunately, I had kept cruising in mind when selecting the Bear and this helped a lot. But the best I could do at this point was to diagram a stowage plan keeping the heaviest items balanced and centered in the boat. I couldn't seriously commit myself to the project until school was out.

Middle school is very demanding, it's more of a life style than a job, and the busiest time is always the last month of the school year. In what seemed like forever, each day felt like a week. Finally, the report cards and student records were completed. The students had left for the summer and I had removed everything of mine from the classroom. Now I was free to go with a paycheck in hand and off into a great adventure.

About a year before taking my sabbatical leave, I had bought a smaller boat. Saying it was "small" is a relative thing compared to the thirty-two- foot schooner my wife and I had just sold. Spending more time sailing with less boat work had become important, so I chose a Bear class sloop to replace the schooner. It's a very attractive one-design boat used for family weekending and racing.

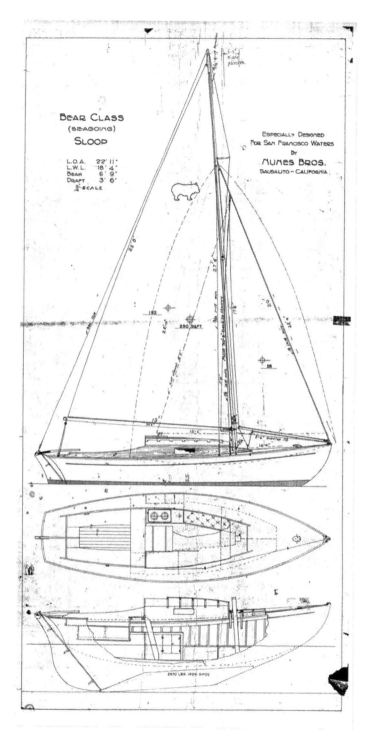

Bears are twenty-three-feet long, with a beam of six feet nine inches, with a three foot, six-inch draft, and two hundred and fifty square feet of sail area. The first one was launched in 1931 from the Nunes Brothers Boat Yard in Sausalito, California. Most of the Bears were built with Douglas Fir planking over oak frames. Built in this manner, they've stood up to over fifty years of hard racing on San Francisco Bay, a bay which has a history of high winds, fast currents, and rough conditions.

During the late 1950's Bears had become the largest one design class on San Francisco Bay. Once you've sailed one, it's easy to see how these boats became so popular. They are exceptional sailers. I first began racing on Bears as crew, usually doing the foredeck. When the opportunity came after a race, I would often take the tiller and sail the boat back to its berth.

It wasn't long before I was racing my own Bear. She was launched as Renegade in 1947 when I was just five-years old. It was a good name for a Bear considering she had an inboard engine when other Bears didn't, but I came to call her Dancing Bear, which seemed to me a friendlier name.

Finding my Bear was no easy task. After looking at five other Bears, I wasn't having much luck. In desperation, I went to see Pete, the foreman of a local boat yard. Leaning over, I knocked on the cabin top of his Atkin designed ketch he kept in Pelican Harbor.

"Hey Pete, you there?" I said.

"Yah, come aboard. What's up?"

"I'm looking for a Bear. You know of any for sale?"

"There's one. I'll show it to you." We went topside and he pointed out toward the anchorage crowded with moored boats. "That's a good one," he said. As I looked at her, she sat gracefully on her lines with a nice aft rake to her mast with swept back spreaders, immediately giving a better impression than the other Bears I'd already seen.

"I'll give you Karl's phone number," Pete said. "Call him, he's a good guy and has been trying to sell his boat for some time now." Karl answered in a gruff voice but he warmed up a bit as we talked about the Bear. To Karl the Bear was Misha. He told me that his kids had grown up on the boat and it had fond memories for him.

"Come on down and we'll talk about the boat some more," he said. Then he gave me his address, which was in the industrial part of the city. I told him I'd drop by the following afternoon. After hunting down parking, I walked to Karl's loft.

It was a very nondescript place easily blending in with its well-worn surroundings. After ringing the bell and climbing the dark creaky staircase, I stepped into a large dimly lit loft cluttered with props that Karl used in his fashion photography business. The far corner, sectioned off with moveable screens, served as his living area.

Although not as tall as me, Karl was a large man with dark hair, and when we shook hands his strength was quite noticeable. He was not a man you'd want to tussle with.

"Well," I said lightly to cover my nervousness," I'm here to see a man about a boat."

"Then let's get down to business. I want $ 4,500 for the boat and will not take anything less for it." After a brief moment of quiet tension, I replied, "I'll have to see the boat first and I want to have it surveyed. Can we arrange a time for that?"

"I haven't got time right now, but I'll give you the key so you can see the boat for yourself. Why don't you take it for a sail while you're there."

"You'd trust me with your boat?" Before answering, Karl's expression changed slightly to one of embarrassment, then with a quick wink and a smile, said, "I've been doing a little checking on you. Well, you don't just sell a Bear to anyone!" He said defensively.

"I'm honored that you trust me. I'll be very careful with her. By the way, how do I get out to her? I know she's on a mooring."

"You'll find a skiff with a dark blue cover on it tied behind the Chinese restaurant next to the boat ramp, a friend lets me keep it there."

(Hmm,) I thought, thinking about the phrase, "Behind the Chinese restaurant," it sounds like something from a murder mystery.

3 FINDING MY BEAR

On a golden afternoon in late fall, a year before the cruise to Mexico, I headed north over the Golden Gate Bridge to Sausalito. Stepping from the van in the parking lot, a cool breeze blew out over the anchorage. It was a good day for sailing. Not far ahead, along the bicycle path, the little skiff with the blue cover lay hidden behind the Chinese restaurant. Looking down from the wharf above, the skiff was side-tied to a small dilapidated float. A short ladder led down to the float below. It failed to reach by four feet. The tide was out. Jumping, I landed lightly next to the skiff.

Would this Bear be like all the others? I certainly hoped not. Slowly rowing around her, it was hard not to notice the missing four feet of toe rail that Karl said had been taken off by a passing fishing boat. That gave her a neglected appearance similar to some of the other boats moored close by. Climbing aboard and sitting, my hand gently ran over her cockpit combing. "Hello little Bear," I said quietly. My eyes traced over her rigging down to her chain plates then followed the line of her shear aft. Other than a few minor details topside, it was obvious that she was in fair sailing condition. Sliding the hatch open I ducked below. She smelled fresh, unlike some of the other Bears that foretold of rot. Although neglected and in great need of paint and varnish, her interior was quite detailed and perfectly set up for my needs.

Fitting neatly under her raised bridge deck were compartments for dishes, cups, knives, and forks. On the port side was a deep stainless sink with a spigot and a pump to drain the sink through the transom. As I investigated further, I found supports for an engine that had been removed long ago. The fuel tank was still in the boat.

After rigging the boat and securing the skiff to the mooring, I waited for the right moment before backing the jib and dropping the mooring line. As she swung clear of the other boats, I walked back to the cockpit.

I always use the term "we" in reference to the boat when sailing. It is a sign of respect. Wooden boats, in my point of view, have a living quality about them. This is due to the effort that builders put into them. They're built with pride and craftsmanship, one piece at a time. That history stays with the boat and must be respected. Wooden boats are different from the majority of boats seen today, which, after being launched from an oil can, are put together by workers on an assembly line.

Being aboard Bear thirty-five, which is her assigned racing number, was remarkable right from the start. She gave a good sense of speed, the kind that gives confidence when another Bear is on your windward quarter less than a boat length away. Responding quickly to my every command, we easily tacked through the crowded mooring field. This Bear didn't do anything half-heartedly. She had her opinions about how sailing should be done and let me know it.

Once out on the bay, she reached her full stride, an easy 5 to 6 knots, reaching on the northwest breeze toward Alcatraz, known to tourists as "The Rock." She loved stretching her legs. The sails were trimmed in and we headed to windward toward the Gate. At the first wave, spray rebounded off the foot of the jib and rattled down onto the foredeck. Normal stuff for summer sailing on San Francisco Bay. The main was slacked until the helm balanced and she sailed herself. Seeing there wasn't any immediate traffic, I ducked below to check the bilge and other areas for leaking. Both the mast collar and fore hatch were leaking along with the lee corner of the cabin trunk. The bilge was wet but holding its own.

Sitting on the windward bunk, I paused and listened to her hard at work. They were good sounds and pleasant to listen to, the swish of the bow wave along the hull, the rattle of spray on deck, accompanied by the constant hum of the wind in the rigging. I was pleased. Going topside, I tacked the boat and headed back toward Sausalito.

It's a complicated thing, a man's relationship with his boat. It's difficult to explain, but the Bear let me know right off that we would work well together. She just had that way about her. It couldn't be defined, but there it was, that concise feeling of speed and responsiveness that didn't have to be coaxed out of her. She spoke to me softly through her tiller. I was in love. It was clear, that she'd had some very competent skippers in the past.

The following week the boat was surveyed, coming through with flying colors except for a crack in the rudder and some other minor work. With the survey completed, I went to see Karl with the intention of buying the boat and skiff.

"There's something you need to know about this boat," Karl said in a dark mood. "She likes to toss her people overboard."

"You can't be serious," I said, laughing in disbelief.

"No, I'm very serious." His expression darkened further as he spoke, lowering his voice as if he were afraid we might be overheard, "I was sailing alone, headed out under the Golden Gate. The boat was sailing herself when I went forward to tension the main halyard. Without knowing how, I suddenly found myself in the water grappling with the boat as she swept by.

At the very last moment I was just able to grab the backstay and pull myself aboard. It all happened so quickly!"

After a lengthy silence we spoke no more of the matter. I paid him for the boat. We shook hands and I was on my way. Although I had handled more demanding boats in the past, it still made me consider Karl's story and question if I were truly up to sailing this Bear, especially one with a dark side. However, I had great confidence in myself, and after awhile passed it off as a freak accident that would probably never happen again. At least not to me, and especially not on my Bear.

It was now June 13th, nine months after buying the Bear, and I was scheduled to sail out under the Golden Gate no later than mid-October. That didn't leave a lot of time to get the boat ready considering that everything from the masthead down to the keel had to be checked, repaired, or replaced. People often spend years outfitting their boats, getting them ready for a cruise. Even so, some still don't make it. It takes money and real commitment to make a cruise happen.

My old Volkswagen van, loaded with a cargo of boat supplies, coasted easily to a stop in the dirt parking lot. She was tired and had not shown much enthusiasm lately, complaining about ailments brought on by her several hundred thousand miles of loyal service. I gave her an affectionate pat on the dash to encourage her, knowing that she still had several months of hard work ahead.

The door of the van slid open to a beautiful summer day in Sausalito. San Francisco, on the other hand, was shrouded in fog with only the tops of its tallest buildings reaching up into the sunshine.

It was a bit of a challenge rowing out to the Bear's mooring with a load of supplies that restricted my movement. Once on board, I couldn't help but admire the panoramic view of the bay crowded with boats. It was so much better than being inside the yacht harbor.

The busy day flew by in no time. As the sun set behind fog capped hills, I was satisfied with what I had accomplished. Everything aboard the Bear had been off loaded, and all the cabin furniture built as separate modules were now in the van. Those boat parts in the van would all have to be refinished, but not being very realistic at the time, I told myself that I could do that at night in my small apartment.

As the work progressed, concerned friends would often ask, how can you possibly work out there on that mooring? You don't have any electricity, as though to them, it was a permanent barrier to any progress. Had they failed to notice my finger tips? As I worked, they were wrapped in masking tape because the skin had long ago been worn off from constant sanding.

Just when help was needed the most, Tony Gaetani volunteered, offering his shop as a place to work. Tony ran a successful construction business in the city. He had been a friend for a long time, but it was only lately that he had learned to sail, so I took him under my wing, so to speak, just to show him the ropes. Now, he felt it was his turn to do the same for me.

Fortunately for me, the timing was good. His shop was clear and all his projects were on-site. He only used the shop for custom work, such as cabinets for kitchens and French doors with beveled glass to please his wealthy patrons.

Meanwhile, the interior refinishing continued on the boat full time. I also began building small projects at his shop on my way home. Often after a day of painting or varnishing aboard the Bear, I'd return to the shop to sand, paint, and varnish some more. That was the routine I stuck with until all the interior projects were finished.

Then came the fun part, installing all the refinished modules that had been removed earlier. Now it was easy to see the value of the work I had done. The Bear looked like a new boat! But there was still a lot more to do. I was running out of time in spite of never taking a day off and often working well into the night.

I told Tony about it and he offered to build a box for the rear half of the cockpit. This box would hold the Avon inflatable dinghy and a solar panel to charge a battery. The Bear's standard cockpit was too large for ocean cruising. Even with the larger drains I had installed, they still couldn't empty the water out fast enough. Once the box was in place, the cockpit was less than half its original size and felt very secure.

Most of the equipment needed for ocean cruising and living aboard had been ordered earlier. These were basic items that most cruising boats have: a new mainsail, dodger, sun awning, two clothes bags, wind vane, bow roller, chart bag, and numerous other small things which added up to more than I had paid for the boat.

It was time to move aboard the boat. I emptied out my apartment in Pacifica, which didn't amount to much, and returned most of its contents to my wife who would find them more useful than I had.

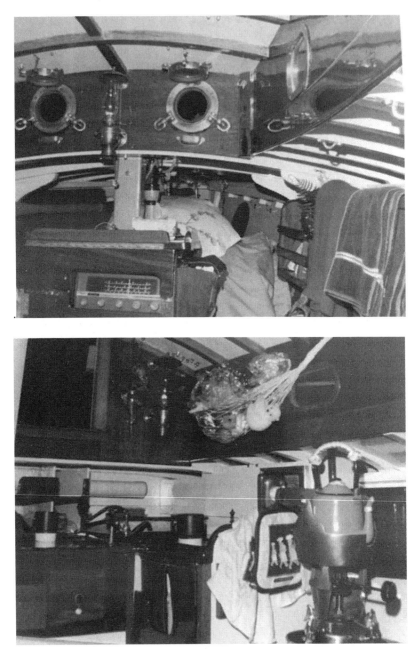

This was not the first time I had lived aboard so the adjustment was an easy one. In fact, I had been looking forward to it for quite some time. The Bear just felt like home.

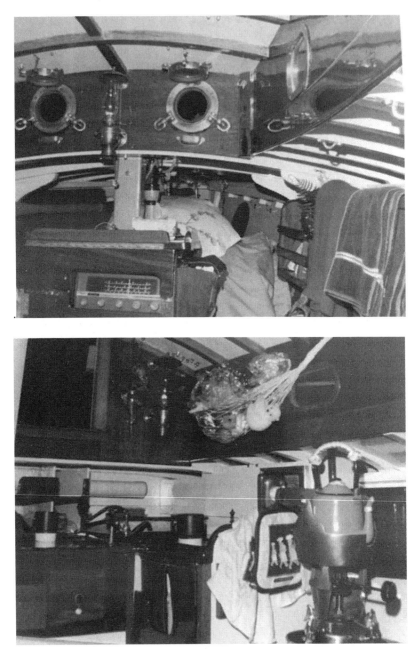

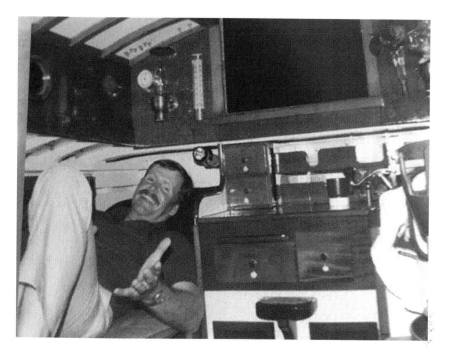

Going below and lighting the lamps, feeling their warmth, and seeing the reflected light play off the fresh varnish and polished brass was perfect.

September was the season of Indian Summer. The cold fog and high winds of summer had all but disappeared. The evenings were spectacular with the sparkling lights of the city's skyline across the bay and the nearby Sausalito waterfront, which were all easily seen from the Bear's cockpit. It was quite peaceful living on my mooring in Richardson Bay.

The skiff was now kept at the Sausalito Cruising Club a short distance from my mooring. The club also provided a nice social setting as well as a shower, and parking for the van.

As October arrived the Bear was sailed to Sven's boat yard in Alameda. Once the boat was hauled at Sven's, the hull's topside paint was removed and the seams were re-caulked. The hull was faired and she was given two coats of primer and finished with two coats of white gloss.

The taxi yellow cove stripe that ran below the boat's shear was a nice accent, painted free hand with a sign painter's brush. A navy blue stripe, called a boot top, was also added just above the light blue bottom paint to set off the white hull. As a final touch, I painted Dancing Bear's name on the stern. The work was finally finished, but much later than expected.

Normally that wouldn't have been a problem, but I had scheduled a Bon Voyage party with my family and friends for the following day in Sausalito. If it weren't for the party, I wouldn't consider sailing the bay at night, but under the circumstances was forced to. It was late afternoon before we finally got away. The tide had turned against us, but I set sail anyway, thinking this would be a good shakedown for what was to come.

Three hours later we were still on the estuary, slowly being swept backwards toward the boat yard by the full force of the flood tide. A fisherman on a nearby pier yelled out across the water just as the sun set. "Hey, you got no wind. Sorry for you!"

That didn't make me feel any better, but dinner was made while I sailed on as best I could. As the evening matured, the breeze began to freshen before we cleared the estuary at midnight. An hour later we passed under the Bay Bridge. Engaging the vane, I went below and laid in a course for the southeast end of Angel Island hoping to slip across the shipping channel without conflict.

Coming topside a short time later, all I could see was fog and a few unfamiliar lights. With the Bear sailing the course I had penciled on the chart, there was nothing to do but settle in on the lee cockpit bench and try to stay warm.

As we beat to windward the fog thickened. Nodding off occasionally in the cold damp cockpit, I would awaken with a start then admonish myself for not staying awake. It was just after being lulled almost to the point of sleep again by the rhythm of the boat, I became aware of a slightly different sound. Listening again, just the breeze over the sails and the rhythmic swish of the bow wave were all that pierced the silence. Settling back deep into the cockpit again, pulling my watch coat tightly around me, I continued my fight to ward off the chilling breeze. All was well.

Experience told me that listening too hard would only lead to imagining what wasn't there. On the other hand, my experience said that every time I had attempted to cross a shipping channel at night or in fog there had been a ship.

As we continued beating to weather, I began to nod off again when something caught my attention. Leaning out to leeward from the dodger, I listened. There it was, just between the swish of the bow waves, the faintest sound of a blaring ship's horn. It was coming from leeward.

Our courses were in conflict!

At that point a light appeared. It surprised me at first, because it wasn't supposed to be there, but there it was the Alcatraz light. The Bear was to windward of my plotted course. In my fatigue, I had forgotten to vector in the lee bow ebb tide. My choices at once became clear, we could continue to beat across the outbound shipping channel in the fog to cross the course of the approaching ship, or we could fall off downwind until the ship had passed, then sail north behind Angel Island and into Raccoon Straits.

The ship's horn was much louder now, but not quite so much as to jump out of the fog and cut us in half, although it certainly felt like it. Anxiously, freeing the tiller and pulling it to windward, the main sheet was let run, sending the Bear off downwind into the unknown darkness.

Every moment was one of heavy suspense. With a dry mouth and sweaty hands, I stood in the cockpit and held our course steady on. Where is that ship? Dead ahead?

Suddenly, the ship materialized through the fog less than two hundred feet away, at first only as a foremast light.

Oh shit, we're closing fast. Which way do I go?

A moment later the ship, became a dim shape marked by its port running light, just visible through the murkiness, as the Bear blissfully sailed on. I watched the ship pass as I stood like a deer in the headlights, frozen to the tiller.

Slowly the ship disappeared back into the fog, giving a parting blast of its horn that vibrated the Bear down to its keel. Then came the long slow rolling wake, just to let us know what we had missed.

After a slow cold sail through Raccoon Strait, we arrived at the Cruising Club about three-thirty in the morning. Once the Bear was tied up and the sails furled, sleep found me as soon as my head hit the pillow. But it was a restless one, as I struggled with troubling dreams about roaming ships in the night.

The following day, the first priority was to clean up the boat. There were many people coming to see the Bear, all trying to imagine how such a small boat could possibly sail all the way to Mexico.

My family was a sailing family and they knew the danger I was facing, but to their credit they never spoke of it. None the less, their tension could be felt, but they, just like everyone else, wanted to give me a good send off and wish me luck. For that I was very grateful, because luck always plays a part when sailing single handed, just as it had the night before. You can't be on watch or at your best twenty-four hours a day.

Now that the work of getting the boat ready was complete, the reality of actually doing the cruise had started to seep in. Had I taken on too much? Dark thoughts occurred. Would this be the last time I see any of these people? But still, the need to press forward, due to the travel study contract and all those who were so supportive, pushed me onward.

It was time to deliver.

A big adventure, was about to begin!

4 OUTWARD BOUND

It was already November seventh, and it was late, very late, to be sailing down the coast. So far the southeast gales had held off and that was good, but they wouldn't for much longer. Experienced voyagers had left months ago and were now in San Diego before heading on to Mexico. They knew this was no time to be cruising along the California coast and so did I.

However, I was driven by my obligation to the contract. And like anyone else who was seriously late, I would be willing to take a chance just like drivers often do when running the last of a yellow light. If I didn't sail now in these deteriorating weather conditions, there would be no travel study. Even considering the possibility that the Bear would be caught in a southeast gale, it was still now or never. My only comfort was that the farther we sailed south the safer we would be, or so I thought.

Just before putting in the hatch slides, I took one last look below. Everything was in order. The log was dated and open with the pencil, parallels, and dividers on the chart table. I locked the hatch and went to breakfast at the local diner. Just as I was paying the check, I noticed Pete sitting at a far table. Wandering over I said hello, mentioning that I was sailing south today and wanted to say good bye.

"You're not leaving now are you? Don't you know there's a storm coming! It's suppose to be here Sunday evening."

"Pete, I'll be in Monterey by then," I said casually. "Don't worry."

But in his concern he continued on. "And look at what you're wearing. Those aren't even sailing clothes."

"Pete this is what I always wear. The foul weather stuff is on the boat."

"Oh. Well ok, but be careful," he said somewhat sheepishly knowing he had over reacted.

After arriving back at the boat, I did a final check before raising the mainsail, which luffed gently in the morning breeze. There would be an ebb tide under the Gate in about an hour. My anxious mind was racing full of "what ifs", but it was time to go. Tony was already out there sailing around waiting to escort the Bear out under the Gate. This had been prearranged during the Bon Voyage party. I took in my lines and pushed off. The mainsail was run out and we moved off down the fairway toward the bay at a good pace, leaving the Cruising Club behind with the Cass Marina's rental sloops rocking gently in our wake.

Looking back over my shoulder, I burned that glance into my memory and wondered how long it would be before I returned. Coming around onto a close reach, I secured the tiller and went forward to raise the jib, making sure that the halyard was carefully coiled and hung tightly on its cleat. It was a beautiful day. There was no fog anywhere and the wind was filling in nicely. Tony sailed over with his girl friend, Jenny, and some other friends aboard his Vanguard 33, Escape. We yelled back and forth as our courses converged and occupied ourselves by taking lots of pictures.

It didn't take long to slip out the Gate with a nice breeze drawing us ahead and a good ebb tide pushing. I was some distance ahead of Tony when he suddenly turned back toward the bay. Wondering why, I glanced around. The fog that had been just a fringe on the horizon a short time ago was now rapidly coming in, blotting out everything. I was truly on my own and sensed the urgency of it. But that was quickly forgotten in the rush to establish a fix. Grabbing a scrap of paper and the hand bearing compass, bearings were taken on the north tower of the bridge, Mile Rock, and just before it was covered in fog, the Point Bonita light.

Down below, with the vane sailing the boat, the bearings were quickly plotted on the chart with a sharp pencil. Where they all intersected was my fixed position and point of departure. After quickly checking the heading on the sailing compass in the cockpit, the magnetic heading was corrected for variation and deviation then drawn as a line on the chart from my fixed position.

That line was our new course.

The mileage from the Sum Log was recorded in the log book as our point of departure. Coming up on deck found us sailing in a world of grey at five knots over a gentle swell. It would have been nice to have seen the Cliff House, Seal Rocks, and San Francisco where I grew up, but that was not possible in the fog. As we crossed the southern bar, I worried about the large waves that broke offshore in the fall and winter. Those waves had taken many lives and boats, and in this fog I wouldn't have any warning if they were breaking.

Later that afternoon the fog began to lift, exposing the Montara lighthouse off the port bow. This gave me an opportunity to work a distance off with a series of bearings on the lighthouse to affirm our position.

As the fog continued its retreat, the deeply colored sunset began to slowly fade into twilight taking the wind with it, leaving us bobbing about with slating sails and the boat pointing in the wrong direction.

Sailing into Half Moon Bay had been part of the original plan, but the wind just wasn't there for that. Being quite disappointed, I turned the Bear south toward Monterey in the first zephyrs of a new evening breeze. It was a new experience for me, being forced to sail through the night rather than conveniently gliding into a harbor just before sunset.

Preparing for the coming night, dinner was made and cleared as I continued to keep a watch for traffic. Slowly, the wind began to increase as the last of the dishes were put away, bringing our speed up to about five and a half knots.

The cabin lamps that had been lit for some time chased out the invading darkness, providing the familiar comfort of home. A lovely three quarter moon lit our way. It was a beautiful evening for sailing and a nice start for our first night at sea. However, we were interrupted as a north bound ship suddenly broke out of what I thought to be a distant fog bank, disrupting the serenity of our pleasant evening, passing less than a quarter of a mile away. I had seen lights ahead earlier, but assumed they were just traffic along the coast highway. Were those the lights of the passing ship that I had so easily dismissed as road traffic? It was strange that the ship hadn't sounded a signal in the fog. This incident was disturbing and I resolved hereafter not to take anything for granted.

About midnight, the Pigeon Point Light came into view. Taking several bearings soon confirmed our position. In the early morning, the moon sank into the fog offshore and it became very dark. However, I was still just able to make out the jib in the starlight. I amused myself with sailing the Bear by the stars rather than using the compass or vane until it got too cold. Putting the vane back to work, I retreated below to check my position and warm up.

Just as I had finished there was a loud crash! We had hit something.

The boat lurched sideways. I raced up into the cockpit. There was nothing to see in the blackness. Later, before daylight, two ships and a fishing boat passed offshore headed north.

About an hour before daylight we headed in toward Monterey. Just the idea of sailing into Monterey on a quick reach with the sun coming up made me feel good. But it was not to be. The wind veered into the east, quickly building to twenty knots. Slowly, the sun appeared as a orange ball, fighting its way up through the thick Salinas Valley fog in the east. Watching its progress, I sat on the galley counter eating oatmeal for breakfast while peering out from under the protection of the dodger. Spray, driven by the wind, rattled off the mainsail overhead before being whipped off to leeward into a cold impersonal sea.

I wasn't happy. "So this is how it is, not at all like the dream," I thought sarcastically. "Shut up and eat your oatmeal. Oh look, the bilge is filling up. What fun! Now it's time to bail."

My earlier efforts at fixing those fore hatch leaks were no match for the waves bringing so much water onboard. Even more interesting were the six foot swells still coming in from the Pacific against this new wind. Maybe they were a forerunner of the coming gale that Pete had mentioned, but I doubted it. It was a very strange experience to be beating to windward as the Bear surfed down the large swells that were overtaking us from astern. The wind and sea began to moderate as we continued to close the distance with Monterey. Making a note of where the leaks were, I swore to fix them once and for all. It was mid-morning before we finally arrived off Monterey.

My foul weather gear that had been worn all night just to keep out the cold and damp was now draped about the cockpit drying. The scene was idyllic. Warm sunshine permeated everything. Lots of boats were out sailing which lifted my spirits as I watched them. It was difficult to keep an eye open and avoid all the traffic after such a sleepless night. As we neared the harbor entrance, the jib was lowered and the coil for the main halyard was removed from its cleat and laid on deck to run free the instant the main needed to be dropped. Back in the cockpit, the docking lines and fenders were also made ready.

"Here we go," I thought anxiously as the wind vane was disengaged. It had been years since I had last been in this harbor. Not being sure where to go, I headed in hoping for the best. The Bear stalled right in the narrowest part of the entrance where the wind was blocked, creating a minor traffic jam, but those behind me were patient and seemed to take it well. Avoiding all the dead ends and wrong turns, we sailed directly to the Monterey Peninsula Yacht Club, just as though the Bear had always known the way. After getting permission to leave the boat temporarily, I went to see the port captain for a berth.

Raising the main again, we sailed to our new berth, a windward one, and a great location for watching the tourists who had come for the day. Once settled in, after a twenty hour watch at sea, it was the bunk that beckoned most.

The first short leg of a long voyage was safely completed.

I became concerned about the coming gale and how long we would be weather bound. The following day l checked the weather, the gale wouldn't arrive until late in the day. This would give me the time needed to fix the leaks and make other improvements.

Finding my way to the local fisherman's supply, which was once the old railroad depot, I purchased some parachute cord and a roll of duct tape. The duct tape sealed all the leaks. Of course that's not the proper way to do it, but both time and money were in short supply.

Then, after setting up the bosun's chair and going up the mast, the parachute cord was used to make the lazy jacks that would capture the mainsail when it was lowered or reefed. The idea behind it was to reduce the time spent on deck for safety reasons when reefing or furling sail.

The sky clouded over by late afternoon and it began to drizzle. Seeing this coming beforehand, the awning was already rigged and I was enjoying a glass of wine with a good book in the cockpit. It was such a pleasure to hear the rain rattling off the awning, knowing that I was dry and secure.

During the night the gale arrived with high winds and more rain. Snuggling deeper into my sleeping bag, I made good work of catching up on sleep. The power of the storm was quite impressive. The following morning, it was interesting to watch several commercial jet liners buck the gale, crabbing along on their incoming flight paths as they flew over the harbor. Later that day, there was a break in the weather. The rain stopped temporarily, but it was still blowing hard.

I was on the dock checking my lines when a gentleman with graying hair approached me. He had been working on his boat when I sailed in the day before. Having a Bear himself, he was curious about mine and wanted to know my plans. He listened closely as I spoke while I watched for his reaction.

People's expressions often give away what they really think. Others who had previously asked questions about the cruise had opinions that ranged from "what a great idea," to "are you out of your mind?" "I would never do that!" However, the Bear skipper seemed to be supportive, but was opposed to my sailing around Point Conception alone and suggested that I take a crew.

The only thing I knew about Point Conception was its reputation for being the grave yard of the Pacific. There was a story that had been passed around about a yacht that had gone missing off Point Conception. It had probably been run down by a ship. All that was found were pieces of the boat and half a body.

Point Conception seemed a long way off to me, so I said that I'd think about it, but I had no intention of putting anyone else through such an ordeal. I offered to show him the boat and he carefully looked it over. Then he invited me to meet his family and have dinner.

That evening as the gale continued to blow, I listened to the Radio Direction Finder just to catch the local news for entertainment. Two reports told about Coast Guard rescues that captured my attention. The first report was about a person moving his twenty-five foot sloop from Moss Landing to Santa Cruz during the gale. The boat was taking on more water than the skipper could bail. The Coast Guard rescued him after a long search that made the news for several days. The second report involved a power boat, also about 25 feet, with two surfers aboard. The Coast Guard failed to find them in the stormy darkness. In their last conversation with the Coast Guard, the surfers said their boat was going down. They put on their wet suits, got on their surf boards, and abandoned their boat. They survived a long paddle to shore and showed up the following day.

A close watch was kept on the weather radio. There were a series of gales coming through with minor breaks in between. This went on for ten days giving me time to play the tourist. I've always been interested in history and used the time between storms to my advantage, taking walking tours to historic buildings and learning as much as I could about Monterey's past.

Clarence and Adrian Du Barrows arrived on Turtle, their Tahiti Ketch, during a break between storms. I had first met them in Sausalito when Clarence was running the Sausalito Marine Ways. I was out sailing when a large power boat ran over my mooring, dragging it in front of the marine railway. Clarence was not happy. Finally, with help, I was able to move the mooring. Since that time, we've been good friends. It was good to see them again and have some connection with the world I had left behind.

The weather was improving and I knew a weather window would need to be chosen soon for our escape down the coast. The next safe harbor was Morro Bay. It was a long sail south, along a rugged coastline that offered little protection.

Would the Bear be able to make that sail safely? I didn't know for sure. It all came down to the skill of picking the right time to sail and luck with the weather.

5 SAILING THROUGH THE WINDOWS

The thought of going back to sea was difficult for me; there was danger out there. The gales had set in and if my luck held, we would be able to safely sail through fair weather windows on our way south. Bears are tough little boats, able to stand up to a lot of abuse, but if it comes down to it, it's best to pick those fights wisely.

Finally, on Wednesday, November 18th, we left Monterey. We had our weather window. Sailing out of the berth was easy enough, but we were becalmed as we attempted the narrow entrance, then headed by a breeze with no room to tack. I had the scull oar ready which helped. But I still had to push off from the last of the piles in the entrance until we squeezed out of the harbor.

The boat handled beautifully, tacking quickly through the last of the moored boats under a sky filled with puffy white clouds casting dark shadows that raced over what remained of the stormy white capped water. The Bear's lee rail quickly submerged once we sailed beyond the protection of the breakwater. It was clear a reef was needed. After clipping my lifeline onto the jack line that ran, fore and aft along the deck, I went forward. Fortunately I had the foresight to put on my foul weather gear. It was wet up there. Reefing the main took only a minute, thanks to the lazy jacks that helped secure the bunt of the sail along the boom.

Once back in the cockpit, I watched the Bear as she settled into the groove making easy work of the windward beat. The sea buoy could just be made out on the ragged edge of the distant horizon. Down below, braced against the heeling boat, a southerly course was plotted from the outer sea buoy as spray rattled down on the cabin top. At the buoy, the log was read and we took our departure south. "Well, here goes nothing," I thought. "Who knows what's going to happen, but I've got to make a start."

The wind vane had been at work for several hours as the Bear ran wing and wing in the rough seas. The vane is a fascinating piece of equipment built of stainless steel and fastened to the boat's deck and stern for support.

At the top of the vane, is a paddle that rotates from vertical to horizontal. It is attached to a dial below that allows the paddle to be turned to face into the wind with a small knob. That knob controls the course the boat sails. Both the paddle and its dial are supported on a tube that stands vertically three feet above its supporting frame behind the rudder. Just forward of the tube is a yoke fastened to the top of the oar whose blade extends several feet into the water. As the blade moves to the right and left, the yoke pulls the steering lines connected to the tiller and steers the boat.

Changing the Bear's course is awkward. To do that, one must climb out of the cockpit, over the life raft box, and onto the stern deck to get to the adjusting knob. Then, by looking forward, you watch the compass in the cockpit and adjust the dial with the knob until the boat steers the correct course. As long as the paddle on top of the vane is pointed into the wind and standing vertical, the boat will sail a course relative to the wind's direction. If the wind shifts, the boat will follow that shift and sail off course. A big part of watch keeping is to check the boat's course, when not watching for traffic. Fortunately, ocean winds are remarkably steady.

It was fascinating just watching the wind vane steer the boat. When running, the boat was often pushed off course by a following sea. The wind direction would change relative to the boat. The paddle, in the vertical position on the top of the vane, would be pushed down until horizontal by the wind moving the linkage from the paddle to a small trim tab underwater on the oar's trailing edge. That tab forced the steering oar to swing out sideways until the pressure between the oar and trim tab are equalized by the force of the moving water. As the oar moves, the steering lines attached to the yoke at the top of the oar move the tiller and correct the course.

The oar was so powerful that it couldn't be overridden manually. However, the wind vane could easily be disconnected by freeing the steering lines at the tiller. Other than the rudder and sails, the vane is the most important piece of sailing gear on the boat.

The seas were a deep blue and about six feet high from the troughs to the crests. Having never sailed the Bear in these conditions, I kept a close eye on the Sum Log, a kind of speedometer that also records mileage. In the present wind, we were doing about five knots in the troughs and sixes and sevens when the Bear surfed on the faces of the seas. This was a safe speed for the conditions. It's important to keep in mind that the faster the Bear goes the less buoyancy she has to lift to following seas.

In the late afternoon, while I was watching for traffic, quite suddenly three north bound Orcas broke through the backs of passing seas about fifty feet off the port side. It was an exciting moment. All those teeth, raw power, and how the closest one aggressively eyed me was a bit scary. Suddenly, the Bear wasn't nearly big enough, and I not nearly as confident as I had been just moments earlier.

All was well until the wind picked up. This increased our speed to sevens and eights. The Bear didn't seem to mind at all, but I thought it was a little fast. A second reef was put in just to slow the boat a bit. That did the trick until the wind dropped in the late afternoon. The reefs were taken out, but even with the added sail area, the Bear slammed about in the remaining waves with the light breeze.

It was interesting watching the vane trying to cope in these conditions. As we came to the top of the swell, the sails would snap forward with the breeze behind us. Then on the face of the sea, the boat would surf forward faster than the breeze bringing the sails aback. This went on for several hours until the vane finally gave up, leaving the Bear rolling in the troughs beam to the seas. At that point, the only thing to be done was to sail the boat myself. Once it got dark the wind began to increase and the vane was able to manage again.

The rest of the night was pretty much routine except for a jibe sometime around midnight. After jibing the jib, I paused on the foredeck leaning back against the mast, admiring a half-moon racing through the clouds above. Looking down, the foredeck was covered with silver droplets reflected in the moonlight. It suddenly occurred to me that this foredeck was a very small one to be standing on. Carefully, I retreated to the safety of the cockpit.

As the navigation lights of other vessels came into view, bearings would be taken and their movements tracked. Also, passing navigational aids were used to update my position with either a running fix or a distance off. All this helped to keep me awake and watchful. Sailing along this busy coast left little time for sleep.

The following day about noon, a school of Dolphins came to play around the boat. They were beautiful to watch, such power and grace. After some concern over my navigation, Point Piedras Blancas came into view and I was able to update my position and lay in a course for San Simeon cove.

It always makes me anxious heading in toward an anchorage when all you can see of it are the waves pounding on cliffs and a rocky shore ahead. You know that the anchorage is there and it will become visible as you close in on it, but relying on your navigation still takes confidence.

Originally, I had planned to make it to Morro Bay. The distance was just too great so I settled for San Simeon cove instead. It was a risky choice. The cove's entrance was exposed to southerly gales this time of year, but I had been without sleep for thirty-four hours and needed the rest.

I found myself thinking about the two boats that had sailed into Monterey during the storms that held me there for so long. One was a Tahiti ketch and the other was a Thunderbird class sloop. After inquiring about them, I was told they had been anchored in San Simeon Cove, but were driven out by six-foot breaking waves generated by a southeast gale. It was a narrow escape for them. Once at sea, their only option was to seek safety by running with the storm to Monterey.

With the weather still remaining fair and considering my need for sleep, I felt the cove was worth the risk. As I remember, there was good holding ground and we were soon anchored behind a barrier of kelp which afforded some additional protection.

After a solid night's sleep, I was ready to take on the next leg to Morro Bay. We cleared the outer buoy by nine in the morning with patchy fog, a fair wind, and a smooth sea. As the day moved on, we picked up a little more breeze that would occasionally push us up to four or five knots. Because Morro Bay wasn't that distant, it seemed best to sail only a few miles offshore as we continued south. After checking my navigation with a running fix on a buoy off Cambria, I found we were sailing in an opposing current. This slowed our progress. It was already late in the afternoon and that worried me. I didn't want to arrive after dark. Also, the fog that had kept its distance all day was moving in.

Just as we were within a mile of the Morro Bay entrance, tufts of thick fog began to blow by overhead. The race was on to get to the entrance before I lost sight of it. The wind, now only about six knots, wasn't much to work with. The steep ground swells began to rapidly increase in size.

Each swell took its turn with us. Silent and indifferent, they stole our wind, setting us closer to the breakwater with each attempt before crashing on to it with great force, sending spray high over its top. At first, our demise seemed inevitable as we sailed in toward the seemingly unreachable safety of the entrance. However, the Bear fought on valiantly, resisting the best efforts of the swells.

Nursing the Bear along as best I could, I watched terrified at the possibilities failure was sure to bring. If we were swept onto the breakwater, the Bear wouldn't last a minute. I didn't think much of my chances either.

Needy for wind and struggling with the forces against us, everything hung in the balance. Would this cruise end here? The next vital minute would tell. Stubbornly, we continued to skirt the raw edge of disaster, totally dependent on what little wind we could find.

Finally, barely escaping the looming breakwater, we slipped into the safety of the harbor.

That I was relived to get in, is an understatement. I sailed over to the yacht club and rafted up to a replica of Joshua Slocum's Spray, the first boat to be single handed around the world. As soon as the Bear was put shipshape I headed for the yacht club bar.

The bar was quite a surprise. Where I expected a traditional bar to be, there was a full size half model of a shoal draft sailboat with its deck serving as the bar's counter. Unusual as this bar was, it served plenty of what I needed at the moment.

"This is the best place for a single handed sailor to be," I thought, "In a yacht club bar on a Friday night," as I quickly emptied my first drink with a silent toast that said, "Just grateful to be here." It was halfway through my second drink before I began to calm down.

My thoughts were interrupted as Clarence and Adrian came in. We exchanged greetings. They had been worried and expressed their concern about my not showing up earlier. Although still shaken by the sail into Morro Bay, I brushed it off trying to remain my easygoing self and made some remark about the wind being anything but reliable. That night I had dinner with Dick and Barbara who were sailing south in their Hans Christian forty-three, a sturdy double ended cutter. We were joined by Clarence and Adrian who were also on their way to Mexico in Turtle, a fiberglass version of the Tahiti ketch. We had a nice time that evening which helped to relieve the stress of earlier events.

At nine o' clock the following morning, Clarence gave us a tow through thick fog out of the harbor. On the way out, I couldn't help but re-live yesterday's experience, as we dropped into the troughs of the steep oncoming swells still beating heavily against the breakwater. Wishing me luck, Clarence cast me off, before disappearing into the fog as he and Adrian headed off under power toward Point Buchon. I went forward and pulled in the towline then raised the jib. My departure point was plotted from the entrance and noted in the log while the Bear continued to sail herself offshore beyond the reach of the large swells.

Our destination was Avila Beach, about twenty-five miles distant. An hour later, curious about our progress, I attempted to update our position and discovered that the Sum Log had jammed. Removing the cable from the meter, I rotated it backwards and was able to free up the little propeller under the hull. Guessing our estimated speed for the hour the log may have been jammed, I estimated we had sailed about two miles along our course and marked it on the chart with a question mark.

Meanwhile, I kept an eye and a sharp ear out as we ghosted along within the sound of unseen surf, not far off the Point Buchon Peninsula. By one-thirty we were rounding the Point. All was going well, but as we began to approach Avila beach I became more anxious about our position. The wind had increased to twenty knots as we ran through thick fog straight in toward the beach.

I felt like an amateur with a confidence problem, and sailing toward the beach at this speed felt way too risky. Visibility was less than two hundred feet as we surfed at six to eight knots on the faces of the swells. I peered ahead, anxiously attempting to penetrate the fog. The mainsail jibed without warning bending the boom almost to the breaking point before I could release the preventer. After jibing back and sorting everything out, I continued my vigil in the fog.

Just as I considered heading back out to sea for the night, the fog began to lift as we approached the shore. Suddenly, just ahead the beach appeared. In the distance, off to port, the wharf at Avila Beach could just be made out. It was such a relief. The Bear's sails were hauled in and we beat to windward toward the anchorage. Once anchored, the tension began to ease. I took my time putting the boat in order. Turning on the news, I poured myself a glass of wine and settled in.

There was a storm expected later in the evening, with rain and southerly winds up to thirty knots. "I'll sit this one out," I thought. Even though this is an exposed anchorage there is no sense in trying to beat farther down the coast into a storm and it's too late to go back to Morro Bay. I knew the storm would certainly arrive before I could get there, and entry into Morro Bay at night was not an option.

This time we were caught. Avila Beach would not provide the shelter we needed. Climbing into the cockpit, I gazed out at the sea. It had calmed down and the fog had disappeared leaving high clouds, the forerunner of a storm to come. I reasoned that the ground tackle would keep us safe. It had been calm for some time, but as I looked up, the masthead pennant had already began to veer into the south.

Gradually, my thoughts drifted to the day I bought the anchor now holding the boat. I had brought it up to the cash register and was paying for it when a friend, a local sailmaker, said, "You aren't taking that with you!"

Yes, I said. "I plan to use it as my first anchor."

"You're going to use an old fashioned fifty-five pound anchor on a Bear? Where are you going to put it?"

"It'll go on the foredeck with the stock pointing down alongside the hull. All it needs are some good chocks to hold it in place so it's easy to secure when getting underway."

More than once, alone in the blackness of a violent night, with only the big anchor between us and destruction, I would think of this story and be very grateful to have that big anchor.

After supper was finished, I sat back and contemplated the cruise. My conclusion was that I had been lucky so far. I thought about the others who had become victims of the early winter storms; a fifty-two foot yawl, a thirty-six foot sloop, and a thirty-foot motorboat all sunk with a loss of life since I'd sailed out the Gate. A thirty-five foot sport fishing boat was the latest disaster, capsizing in the swells at the Morro Bay entrance. Five people had drowned hours earlier, just about the time we were rounding Point Buchon.

All this information just fueled the tension and dread I was feeling. This cruise wasn't turning out like I had planned. After dropping off to sleep, I awoke about midnight to a light rain and discovered that the wind, a mere five knots of it, had shifted back into the northwest again. It was a good sign.

Just maybe our luck would continue to hold.

6 CAPE HORN OF THE PACIFIC

Caught! We were in the open anchored at Avila Beach with a gale forecast. Fortunately, it was slow to arrive. Several routes of escape were possible. Mine was to continue sailing south to the safety of Santa Barbara. It was risky. Santa Barbara was the most distant of all the options. The second option was to retreat to Morro Bay which was well sheltered, but had a difficult entrance. It was possible we could be weather bound there for some time because of its entrance. The third option was to stay where we were and weather out the storm at Avila Beach, which was quite exposed.

So far, the weather was still holding, so we took a chance and sailed for Santa Barbara. I chose not to engage the wind vane thinking I could get better performance from the boat. But sailing the boat turned out to be a distraction, blinding me from the unforeseen dangers ahead. As the wind increased, I worried about the coming gale and pushed the Bear hard. When the Sum Log began to register eight to nine knots on the faces of the waves I slowed the Bear by sheeting the jib mid-ships.

I had often read about mariners who had struggled with sailing around points of land and the respect they had for such headlands. That should have provided all the foresight I needed. But somehow, subconsciously, I felt none of that applied to me. After all, I was sailing downwind. So by denying the experience of others, it would have to be learned the hard way.

The closer we drew to Point Arguello, now partially covered in mist from the heavy surf at its base, the more challenging everything became. That mist, a major clue of what lay ahead, had also been overlooked. My strategy was to slip by Arguello and Conception with as little fuss as possible. The real threat, as I saw it, was being caught by the incoming gale. My full attention was focused on sailing the boat south as fast as possible.

29

Unknown to me, the struggle to sail past these headlands had just begun!

As I sat in the cockpit looking aft, I had to lean back to see the tops of the waves coming up from astern. How could the wind and waves have doubled in size so quickly? We were sailing way too fast in these new conditions. Our bow wave had progressively moved aft to the shrouds, shooting up the sides of the hull as high as the cabin top, leaving the Bear's bow extended out beyond the wave face as she surfed the steep crests. However, even in these conditions the Bear remained steady on the tiller as she continued sailing with a full main and jib sheeted in flat.

My panic shifted to fear as I begin to realize what was happening. We should have reefed an hour ago, now we were in way too deep! This was serious trouble, but I could do nothing about it. I was stuck at the tiller. To make matters much worse, we couldn't clear Point Arguello without jibing. Tacking around to avoid a jibe in these conditions was out of the question. The surrounding scene was so horrific I couldn't even begin to imagine trying it. Meanwhile, we were quickly closing in on Point Arguello .

Just as all this was dawning on me, a rogue wave larger than any of the others quickly overtook us. It was steep. The bow went down, then under. Water shot up the side decks around the cabin. The wave's breaking crest tumbled aboard from astern colliding with the water sweeping aft, temporarily submerging the hull in broken water, leaving just the cabin above the surface. I stood dumbfounded in the cockpit with a tight grip on the tiller trying to figure out what to do next.

Instinct overrode my confusion. The tiller was pushed to the lee and the Bear's bow popped above the surface and began surfing the crest of the rogue. My eyes locked on the Sum Log. Eight, nine, then pegged at ten before the final thrust of the wave threw the Bear forward, doubling her designed hull speed.

I finally came to my senses. I would have to go head to head with these conditions if we were to survive Point Arguello. I climbed up over the box that held the inflatable and onto the stern deck while sailing the Bear facing backwards.

There was so much that could go wrong with this plan.

It was a reckless move on my part, but I could see no other choice, even when my expectations for success were zero. I held a death grip on the back stay, which flexed with every shift of my weight, guiding the tiller with my knee. My free hand quickly adjusted the vane. Nothing could be done for the Bear until the vane was engaged.

Seconds later, I was amazed to find myself back in the cockpit having completed the task. The vane now sailed the boat as I hovered over the tiller, just in case it couldn't. Good! The vane can handle it.

No time to waste.

"Come on move!" I yelled at myself. "Get up there and reef the main." Finding myself on the foredeck in a complete adrenaline rush, I released the halyard.

Nothing.

Reaching up, I tugged hard on the main.

Still, nothing.

It wouldn't budge. Too much wind.

In desperation, I grabbed at the luff of the sail with both hands pulling down hard, lifting myself up off the deck. Wrapping my legs around the mast under the boom gave me leverage. Slowly, the sail stubbornly begin to inch down, becoming easier as our sail area decreased. After tying in a double reef, I quickly glanced down toward the bow. It was completely out of the water back to the mast as we continued surfing the steep wave faces.

Hanging ten came to mind. We were certainly getting air under the hull, but these were crazy scattered thoughts just generated by adrenaline. Back in the cockpit again, I checked the Sum Log. The speed was down to a manageable pace with sevens and eights. Ok, one problem solved. Now, time to jibe.

Looking at the sea again, I searched for another way out. But it was no good. Our situation was similar to a condemned prisoner looking for a brightly lit exit sign, while being marched to the execution wall. I thought of dropping the main altogether, but it was too late for that. The headland was much closer. It was not possible to weather it under jib alone.

The boat must be jibed!

Grabbing the mainsheet and pulling it in had no effect. It wouldn't budge either. There was too much wind in the sail, even with the double reef.

Using both feet against the cabin trunk for leverage did the trick and the mainsail slowly began to come in. While pulling in the main, I thought about the weakness all Bears have for catching their booms on the backstay when they lift during a jibe. If that were to happen in these conditions the backstay would surely carry away taking the mast with it. An image quickly flashed through my mind of helplessly drifting toward the lee shore in a dismasted boat, then into the high surf pounding under the steep cliffs which offered little chance of escape.

Stopping to think for a moment, I disengaged the wind vane at the tiller. Continuing to pull in the mainsheet with both hands, I steered the boat with my butt. All was ready, and at the right moment the tiller was pushed over. I had no idea if we would survive this jibe or not. But it was the only way out of this mess. During the fraction of a second it took for the mainsheet to go slack, I yanked down hard on it.

Instantly it was ripped from my hands.

The power of the wind violently slammed the mainsail to the other side of the boat.

The Bear staggered under the impact. Broaching, we skidded into the trough of the next approaching wave. Handling the boat, with both hands on the tiller, the broach was countered before the next wave overtook us and the Bear held to her course.

With a quick glance, I stood looking up at the rig, amazed that it was still standing. The Bear, now headed offshore, was clear to sail beyond Point Arguello.

It had been a desperate struggle! I had learned a lot and came to a firm conclusion that without further improvement, this would not be our last brush with death or destruction. After all, how much luck can one skipper have? That thought left me with a feeling of dread, well deserved, considering my poor performance.

It's often said among those who know, that you must hold at least two of three advantages needed to survive in a small boat at sea. The first one is seamanship. The second is a good boat. The third is luck. Any two of them should get you through. This time it was luck and a good boat.

Not wanting to push my unknown quantity of luck any further, I needed to acquire more seamanship in a hurry. My learning curve was already close to vertical as I continued gathering knowledge through experience. I was learning fast, but would it be fast enough?

Whatever gave me the idea I was ready for ocean cruising? At the time I thought twenty years of bay and delta sailing would have been more than enough but it wasn't. "So now what's going to happen," I asked? "Would Divine intervention be required?"

"Perhaps it already has," a stern voice whispered from deep within.

It was late afternoon as the Bear continued to surf the large seas racing south toward Santa Barbara. Just ahead, off to port, Point Conception looked desolate as the setting sun slipped into the copper tinted clouds of the coming gale. There was no doubt the storm wasn't far off. Watching this scene unfold, I felt defeated. I was a trespasser on the ocean, not having earned the right to be here and desperately wanting to be somewhere else. Retreating below to more familiar surroundings, I lit the cabin lamps for a little comfort and warmth, then put the kettle on for something hot to drink.

As I sat watching the motionless kettle in its gimbals, the cabin continued its constant sway and roll around it. Funny, how I hadn't taken the time to notice these things and how the Bear would drop down the face of a wave picking up speed until the water roared along both sides of the hull like "White Thunder," as I came to call it. Then the boat would slow down in the trough of the next wave, bucking and bouncing, while the water made a sort of burbling sound. Then the whole procedure would start again with the Bear rapidly lifting, as if on an elevator, to meet the next crest quickly coming up from astern.

Ahead, on the far horizon, were the first of the offshore oil rig lights shining brightly, welcoming our progress. Both the wind and sea began to ease once we had sailed beyond Point Conception and into its lee. With the horizon clear of traffic, I turned my attention toward making dinner. The wind had now calmed considerably. The double reef was removed after dinner as we continued south on gentle waves and soft winds.

If there was ever a time for the Bear to reveal any weaknesses or dark secrets, it would have been off Point Arguello. She was truly exceptional in her ability to sail so predictably, even after many of the commandments of good seamanship had been violated. So many other boats might have failed to cope under similar circumstances.

In the shelter of the cabin, I began thinking about the legendary Bear and how she came to be during the early 1930's. She was no more than an idea to her founder before being shaped from a block of wood into a half model. Then, after serious review from those with life-long experience, she was developed into the boat I was sailing today. It was magic when I thought about it, compared to the more modern methods of design. No matter which design method was chosen, traditional or modern, the Bear had that untended tweak that made her exceptional, causing one of her creators to exclaim, "That's one Bear of a boat," inadvertently naming her. Perhaps she was not the fastest for her length among the more modern boats, but in my opinion, she was still the best.

Just before midnight I updated our position. We were off Goleta with Santa Barbara not far away. After checking the cruising guide, it suggested Santa Barbara's harbor could be safely entered with caution at night. Sailing in close to the wharf, I carefully avoided the breaking surf mentioned in the guide that was invisible from offshore at night. Once inside the harbor, the transient dock was easy to find. The Bear luffed up in the gentle breeze making a nice landing, the kind you want on a busy Sunday afternoon when everyone is watching.

Feeling pretty good about that, I stepped casually off the boat onto the float, my knees buckled and I promptly fell on my face. Somewhat embarrassed, I looked around to see if anyone was watching. This had never happened before. Had I lost my land legs? Had my near disaster affected me more than I realized? Exhausted, I looked at my watch as I got to my feet. It was four A.M.

The incoming gale had been successfully avoided!

7 LIFE IN SANTA BARBARA

A distant pounding stubbornly penetrated my deep sleep, then rapidly became much louder as I began the long swim back toward consciousness. A sharp voice yelled in the dark, "I've already told you once, now get up to the harbor master's office and pay your slip fee!"

"Alright, alright," I exclaimed. It was 6 A.M. The harbor police watched as I slid the hatch back a few minutes later and stepped onto the dock. The officer closest to me motioned toward the office, as his backup man stood in close for support. Entering the office, I mentioned my experience with the harbor police to the lady at the desk, "Is this normal behavior here?"

"They just overdo it sometimes," the desk clerk said cheerfully, attempting to smooth things over before assigning me to a temporary berth.

Once it was light, I moved Dancing Bear to her new berth and began working on the boat. It took my mind off earlier events. There was a list of small things that needed to be taken care of that would pretty much fill out my day if I took my time. Among other things, lamps needed to be polished and filled with kerosene, the chimneys needed cleaning, and it was time to trim the wicks. Even with the solar panel doing its best, it couldn't keep up with the demands I had placed on it and the battery needed re-charging. Just as I was figuring out how to do that, Bud Branch appeared.

"Bud, what are you doing here?"

"Elaine and I came down to celebrate Thanksgiving with my father. Sue told me you'd be here. We wanted to invite you for Thanksgiving tomorrow."

"Well, I'm glad you're here, and I'd love to come!" We talked for awhile just to catch up.

Bud was a school psychologist and had recommended some resources to help me combat my depression. His wife, Elaine, taught French and German at the high school level. It had been many months since our last visit. We took the battery off the boat and put it in Bud's car for re-charging at a nearby gas station. Then after picking up Elaine, we were off to tour the Santa Barbara Mission. It was such a nice surprise to see Bud and Elaine, thanks to Sue, and it made the day so much better than the one I had previously planned.

After a pleasant day together, the gale arrived late that night. When I woke up just after daylight, it was blowing hard, I couldn't sleep. The Bear had been dancing around in her slip yanking hard against her mooring lines since well before daylight, making me curious about what was going on outside the breakwater. It seemed best to take a look before the rain started. Seeing a crowd standing on high ground above the breakwater, I headed over to see what they were watching.

Large waves were bursting against the outer sea wall sending heavy wind- driven spray down onto the first and second row of boats that heeled with its impact. I asked if this was normal during a gale, and was told this was the first big storm. Returning to the boat, I was very grateful the Bear was well back in the harbor.

It had been some time since I had given serious thought to Sue, my wife of fourteen years. She was part of the reason I was here now. We were separated, which was my choice. My decision had to do with taking charge of my own life instead of abdicating it to her by proxy. Even now, she was still managing my financial affairs while I was gone, but I appreciated that.

Lately, my depression had disappeared, overruled by the heavy demands of just staying alive. I had been making more decisions lately and that felt good. Some people might call this craziness a midlife crisis. "Imagine, a midlife crisis," I thought just before dozing off on my bunk.

A gentle rapping on the cabin top brought me out of a light dreamy sleep. Bud had arrived to take me up to his father's place for Thanksgiving. Having already showered and changed earlier, I was ready. In spite of the holiday, I was forced to dress in my usual sailing duds which were all I had. Khakis, Oxford button down shirt, crew neck sweater, and my heavy yellow float coat with the usual white tennis hat worn for all sailing occasions.

After a drive up some steep hills we arrived at Bud's father's place. As I remember it, the home was older and well maintained with splendid views of the sea, fitting comfortably into its neighboring surroundings. It was a pleasure to meet Dell, Bud's father. He was a man of medium stature with white hair and full of energy, busy every minute. He wasted no time telling me about his life-long service to the Boy's Club, of which he was very proud. He handed me a mug of hot mulled wine to take the chill off and told me to make myself at home while he was busy in the kitchen.

Wandering over to the fireplace, I leaned against the mantle just to soak up some heat which had been in short supply aboard the Bear. Very grateful to be here, I absorbed as much of my surroundings as possible. Moving over to the window after warming up, I looked through the rain-splattered glass out onto the sea, now a deathly gray speckled with tumbling waves. It was blowing hard out there, making it easy to be in here. The dinner, as I remember, was traditional for the holiday and quite good after my meager fare aboard. Before taking my first bite I paused for a moment, just grateful to be there.

The following morning Bud came by to take me out to breakfast on the pier where we were to meet Elaine and Dell. The food was good, much better than the packets of oatmeal heated with hot water that I had daily. After breakfast we went for a walk on the beach. The gale had begin to move on, leaving behind a sky of shredded clouds with patchy sunshine playing on an angry sea. It was low tide, making the walking on the hard sand easy. We took our time investigating the five yachts torn from their exposed moorings and thrown up onto the beach. It was Interesting to see how the water had washed the sand behind the stranded boats creating a barrier that allowed no retreat, so the sea over time could eventually smash them to pieces.

I was sorry to see Bud and Elaine go, but they had to return to work. And I had to return to the sea. There was still a lot of sailing to be done.

It was time to make plans for the sail south to San Diego. Judging from what I had seen of the local harbor police, sailing down the coast from marina to marina didn't appeal, even when the cost of berthing wasn't an issue. An alternative to the marinas was to sail through the Channel Islands and anchor along the way. However, with the passing of the gale, my old nemesis, fog settled in day after day bringing very light winds and low visibility. This was a serious issue. All shipping moving north or south along the west coast moved between me and the islands I was trying to get to. How was I going to safely cross this busy shipping channel in those conditions? It seemed like the best idea for now was to rest up and wait for better weather.

As I waited on the weather, my time was spent exploring the surrounding area on foot and staying away from the harbor police. There always seemed to be some minor violation that took their full attention. The harbor was strict law and order all the way to the point of micro management.

However, it was not so on the other side of Highway 101. It was just the opposite there, especially after dark. It was a place where you needed to stay on your toes, look pissed, and walk quickly. That worked well except one late night while returning from a movie.

The streets were deserted and poorly lit. Halfway up the block a rather suspicious looking character cut across the street in mid block to my side walking toward me. He had a hand in his pocket as though carrying something. Quickly dodging between parked cars, I jogged to the other side of the street. Seeing I wasn't going to be easy, he continued on his way. It's possible that he meant no harm at all, but I didn't want to find out.

I had learned from experience a long time ago in San Francisco, when I had narrowly avoided a robbery and possible stabbing by ducking aboard the large yacht I was crewing on. Looking back through the safety of the locked gate I saw my pursuer watching me as he slipped a knife back into his pocket.

We had been in Santa Barbara for longer than I cared to stay. It was time to take a chance and sail for Santa Cruz Island hoping to pass safely through the shipping traffic unharmed.

I kept asking myself the question, was the danger worth the risk?

8 IMAGES AND ILLUSIONS

After almost two weeks of waiting and one false start, the weather improved. Finally, there was good visibility and a steady breeze. The following morning we sailed for Santa Cruz Island.

The wind was still light, but I had hopes it would soon improve. However, several hours later it just fizzled out, leaving the Bear adrift in the shipping lanes, pointing back towards the harbor. It was the very thing I had hoped to avoid. Fortunately, there were no ships in sight. Perhaps our luck would still hold. As the afternoon wore on, a slight breeze developed from the northwest, slowly building to about twelve knots.

We arrived at Santa Cruz Island shortly after sunset. It seemed as if there might be just enough time to slip into a cove and anchor for the night, but unfortunately we lost our wind as we sailed into the island's lee. With the shorter days of late fall, darkness closed in quickly frustrating any chance of making an anchorage during daylight. Finally a light easterly breeze developed just as a deep orange moon was rising over Santa Barbara. We began ghosting south on the light breeze, following the island's eastern shore and eventually arriving at Ladies Harbor, which could just be made out in the moonlight.

The harbor was nothing more than a large crevasse cutting deep into the steep rolling hills of the island. There was a sloop moored inside, gently pitching and rolling in the surge. The dread of another night's sail tempted me to anchor there, but it was too risky in the darkness. We continued on south. It was quite beautiful with the soft light of the moon playing on the island's shores. After several hours at the helm, part of it struggling to stay awake, Prisoner's Harbor finally came into view off the beam. There was a pier on its south side with a sandy beach forming a nice cove. Although the moorings were vacant at this time of the year, I anchored elsewhere in the cove.

The following morning I was rousted from a deep sleep as the Bear rolled and pitched in swells coming from the east. We were no longer sheltered and the wind started to build during breakfast. I rushed to finish the last of the dishes keeping a close eye on the lee shore less than a hundred feet behind us. It was the season for Santa Ana winds that can blow from the east up to sixty knots with little warning.

Getting the anchor up was a struggle. I hauled the boat to windward with the mainsail up in the increasing wind. The anchor's trip line floated down alongside the hull and was quickly hauled aboard. Grabbing the anchor by its flukes, it was muscled on deck and it into its chocks much like someone would bull dog a steer. The Bear quickly dodged through the empty mooring field and sailed out of the cove.

It was a relief to reach the safety of open water. The wind vane was engaged, freeing me to hoist the jib and clear the foredeck for the coming blow. Just as I had finished placing the coil of jib halyard on its cleat, the wind demanded a reef in the main. Once reefed, we headed toward the southern end of Santa Cruz Island.

It was time for a coffee break. I needed it. Still panting from my exertions, I put the kettle on the stove and sat on the galley counter under the shelter of the dodger where I could monitor our progress. It felt good to hold a warm mug with cold hands.

As we reached south, I noticed other anchored boats with rolling spars in the more exposed coves. I couldn't help wondering how much longer those boats could safely stay there. The morning so far had been quite a challenge. Hopefully, we would be able to clear the south end of the island before things grew much worse.

As it turned out, the Santa Ana winds were a false alarm and never increased much above twenty to twenty-five knots. Sailing at hull speed, the Bear arrived at Smugglers Cove several hours later. Once out of the worst of the wind and waves, we ghosted slowly into the empty anchorage. Protected by the lee of the island, it was much warmer with light winds and sunshine. I had been freezing for the last few weeks in this late fall weather and it was so nice to get a break from it, if only temporarily. I felt as though I had quite enough sailing for awhile and decided to spend the day in the cove. Later, I took a picnic lunch up into the cockpit to soak up some of the sun's warmth and view our beautiful surroundings.

From the foredeck, I visually followed the trip line from its float on the surface down to the anchor buried in white sand thirty feet below. As I looked toward the shore, the cove was fringed by a crescent beach at the foot of a grassy valley. Up from the beach, random trees grew in no particular pattern near an olive grove. At the valley's far upper end, sage increasing covered hills that gradually transitioned into mountains. Beyond the entrance of the cove offshore, Anacapa Island appeared as a fortress on the horizon, surrounded by steep cliffs and a single pointed peak rising above its plateau.

As the afternoon drifted on I caught up on my reading and sleep. Coming on deck after a nap there were fifteen boats anchored around us. They were most likely forced from the more exposed coves just as we were. By evening, the number of anchored boats had doubled.

After dinner I came on deck to stretch just in time to catch a full blood red moon climbing up through the Southern California smog. Someone in the quiet anchorage let out a howl. It was that spectacular. The remainder of the evening was spent in the cockpit enjoying the moon's upward transit before the night's chill drove me down below and into my sleeping bag. Catching up on sleep was one of the best things I could have done. Little did I know how much I would need it in the coming days.

It was early afternoon before we sailed out of Smuggler's Cove. The plan was to do a night passage to Santa Catalina Island, but the wind died as we sailed past Anacapa. Beyond that point, the sailing was slow going in less than two knots of wind over a flat sea. The rest of the afternoon and night were routine until about two in the morning when the wind completely died.

Exhausted, I took the sails down and furled them, planning to drift and get some sleep. After lying down I became anxious about possible traffic and was unable to sleep. Soon the sails were back up and the Bear continued ghosting toward Catalina through the rest of the night and all the following day. I had now been without sleep for well over thirty hours. Still, I pushed on, dismissing the need for rest as the Bear slowly closed with Catalina. It was about ten-thirty the following night when the trouble started.

Sitting quietly in the cockpit I noticed lights all around the Bear. After a closer look, they appeared to be anchor lights, all from classic wooden power boats. All of them had white hulls and varnished teak cabin sides. Their wheel houses were lit with kerosene lamps. "It must be some kind of a club," I thought. I struggled with this for awhile before finally checking my position then dismissing the power boats altogether. Power boats just don't anchor six miles off the northern end of Catalina Island. However, there they were. "Well, I remember thinking, "This is interesting."

I recalled back to the time in South Korea when I stood guard duty completely exhausted after an outing to the Yellow Sea. I had a hunch they'd check the guard. So, trying my best to stay awake after a long day, I forced myself to walk until I fell asleep on my feet and wandered into a ditch. This freaked out my sentry dog. The dog handler is not supposed to fall down. So plan B was conceived. I found a good vantage point on my post then sat down and waited for the Sergeant of the guard.

That's when the first hallucination appeared. Sitting there, I looked to my left. A little red man with a pitchfork was dancing around in circles. It startled me at first. He seemed so real, I started to reach for the Colt 45 on my hip before looking at my sentry dog. He just sat there panting, not even watching. It didn't take long to put two and two together. Relying on my prior experience, I thought, "Those classic boats are just imaginary, just sail right through them, they're not real." Problem solved. But the problem wasn't solved.

Now off on the port side a granite cliff appeared. We were quickly being drawn toward it by some unknown force. The cliff was so close now that I could easily see the tiny black specs in the granite. As I watched, the specs began moving upward with increasing speed to the top of the cliff, suddenly bursting into white doves. "Spectacular!" I thought. This illusion kept re-appearing, and after several re-runs, I settled back in the cockpit just to watch the Bear sail in the moonlight, relived that the hallucinations were over.

Suddenly transfixed, I watched the reflected path of the moonlight on the water shift to the Bear's bow, highlighting our way ahead. The moon's reflection drew the Bear forward along its path, before plunging over the brink not far ahead into an unseen abyss. The mist, in white gossamer strands, blown upward by the force of the plunging water, was highlighted in the surrounding darkness as we continued sailing toward its edge. "No way," I thought! "Now we're sailing off the edge of the earth! Just play along with it. Let's see what happens next." The illusion began repeating itself before we ever reached the abyss. I shook off the hallucination, making it disappear just as quickly as it had come.

We were only a few miles off the northern tip of Catalina Island. It loomed large, darker than the night sky shutting out the stars. The plankton, more brilliant than normal in the darkness, highlighted our gentle wake with a bright green glow. As we ghosted on, I knew we were too close to the island for sleeping. Even the simplest tasks were becoming difficult.

Looking down into the cabin, I was reassured by the warm glow of the kerosene lights. It was just like home I thought, in fact it was home. But it was different. A very attractive lady was preparing dinner just out of sight down below. All this was quite reassuring and her appearance was welcome. It never occurred to me to question how she got there. Not wanting to lose her companionship, I avoided the disappointment of searching for her in the cabin.

As the Bear ghosted past the northern tip of the island, I began urging her forward, hoping to arrive at Isthmus Cove earlier than I knew was physically possible. I battled to stay awake, finally arriving at the cove about four in the morning. What had been planned as an overnight trip to Catalina Island had become a three day sail with very little wind. Our average speed between Santa Cruz and Catalina Islands, according to my navigation, was only 1.4 knots. Late the following morning, I left Isthmus Cove after a short but sound sleep. There was a good breeze which was a great incentive. As I remember, it was quite cold under the grey sky, even with my heavy coat on, making me wish for the kind of the warmth I knew I'd find in Mexico. After coasting along the Catalina shore for what seemed like hours, the Casino at Avalon appeared off in the distance. I really had been looking forward to sailing into Avalon after seeing so many pictures of it in "Sea Magazine" as a boy.

It hadn't changed much from those pictures. The pictures as I remembered them, showed warm summer days with every mooring occupied. However, the harbor now had an austere look about it, under the cover of steel grey clouds blocking any possibility of the sun's warmth. With just six days before Christmas only a handful of boats were occupying the hundred or so available moorings. I sailed over and tied up to a float alongside the wharf a short distance from the port captain's office. The port captain was very helpful and suggested next time I use my VHF rather than coming up to the office. "It's much easier," he said. He was quite surprised to find that I didn't have one.

The port captain provided me with a diagram that made finding my mooring easy. It was just off the Tuna Club. There were additional instructions in the form of a diagram explaining how to moor fore and aft, which was required. Picking up the windward mooring was easy. Then, following the instructions, I found the underwater line that connected the bow and stern moorings. Pulling in the stern mooring ball hand over hand, I slipped my stern line through its ring and brought it back to the Bear. In a matter of minutes all was safe and secure.

Just after putting the finishing touches on a good harbor furl for the mainsail, the kettle came to a boil. I dropped down below for a cup of coffee and to warm up. Now that the boat was secure, it was time to meet my own needs. First up was a shower. The stuff I needed was hastily thrown into the knapsack. After waiting awhile for the launch, I finally stood up on the cockpit seat, blew my fog horn, and waved my arms until the launch skipper got the idea. He was used to receiving all his requests on VHF, I think that's what the port captain called it. Ah, these modern times we live in, imagine that, a small talking radio!

During my shower, cats wearing blue and red paisley neckerchiefs, wandered about on the top edges of the shower stalls peering in where ever there was action. I had never seen anything quite like that. It was most peculiar. Feeling like a new person, I went for a walk along the shoreline and admired the Bear as I passed by. No one else gave her the slightest notice for she was well out of her territory. As I continued my tour, it was easy to see how truly unique Avalon was. Some of the shops, including a restaurant opened up right onto the beach. Most of the houses, I assumed, were vacation homes, quite small, and set close together on narrow streets. Wandering as far as the Casino theater, I found 'Stripes' was playing that evening.

Under broken clouds allowing for some spotty sunshine, I returned to the beachfront restaurant for dinner. The food was good, better than what I had been eating. One does get tired of Dave's "Suckahash", a favorite among my recipes, which usually contained a mix of whatever could be shoved into one pot.

The cats in the theater were quite amusing. They ran up and down the aisles, scooting under the seats, probably hunting for mice or eating bits of food dropped by former patrons before the movie. After the movie, on my way out of the theater, I asked about the cats and was told that they were something like the sacred cows of India. The powers that be in Avalon just liked cats. I went outside with the others and lined up on the dock to catch the last launch out to the boat, calling it a day.

It was warm and sunny the following morning with a nice promise of wind. I was still anxious about the threat of Santa Ana winds. They generated a restless feeling in me, especially after reading an article a few years back about a Santa Ana that destroyed more than two dozen boats at Avalon. It was time to leave. Catalina would not provide adequate shelter if a Santa Ana were to occur. We were soon underway with a nice breeze. I plotted in a course for Oceanside and worked on the log as we sailed, updating its comments section from the past few days.

Just as I had finished, the wind died completely, leaving us drifting several miles off Avalon. To make matters worse the Bear, completely becalmed, was pointed back toward Avalon. Maybe she wanted to stay awhile longer and would be grateful for the time off. "Well damn!" If I knew this was going to happen I wouldn't have left. But there you have it, another lesson learned about what you want and what you get. Come to think of it, I wouldn't exactly say learned, probably experienced is a more accurate word.

Soon a light wind came up. For the first time since leaving our home waters, I set the spinnaker hoping to cross the shipping lanes to Oceanside before darkness. The vane handled the spinnaker easily in the moderate breeze. A pleasant afternoon was spent in the cockpit enjoying the warmth of the sun while on watch.

As twilight came, with the shipping lane behind, I dropped below to prepare an early dinner for the coming night, taking the time to clean up the galley and light the kerosene lamps. Popping up out the hatch occasionally, I scanned the horizon. It was a beautiful night. The stars were impressive, but I mostly stayed below where it was warmer, and after awhile nodded off while sitting on the bunk. I have no idea how long I slept. Not even being aware of having been asleep, I continued to sit and drift with my thoughts.

Finally, it came to me to update our position, check the miles sailed, and figure out where we were along our penciled course line. "We couldn't possibly have made that much progress," I thought as I continued to walk the dividers along the course line. "We're awfully close to the coast. Popping up out of the hatch, I peered into a thick dripping fog, right down on the water. Looking ahead, I could barely make out the spinnaker in the fog. Sensing danger, I gained the deck moving quickly to the bow. Still, nothing could be seen.

But off in the distance was the gentle roar of surf. Detaching the spinnaker pole from the guy, I stowed the pole on the mast and quickly headed for the cockpit. After gathering in the spinnaker's clews, the halyard was freed and the chute rapidly shot down under the boom and into the companionway. Pausing for a moment, I gave thanks for my racing experience that had allowed me to maneuver the boat so quickly. The Bear was sheeted in and headed up to starboard back into deeper water.

Down below, I waded through the spinnaker, reaching the navigation table to plot a new course, but stopped to rethink the situation. The slow rhythmic sound of a horn could just be heard. Was it the horn at the entrance to the harbor? At least I thought it was, or did I just want it to be the horn at the entrance? It was like the siren's call.

At first, I thought all I have to do is track down that horn and sail into the harbor. I checked the chart to see what I was getting into, but it provided very little information being of the wrong scale. I headed in anyway, sailing toward where I thought the sound was coming from. Both the horn and surf got louder, much louder, but I still couldn't make out the entrance to the harbor or if I was to the left or right of it. I was sailing blind without even considering the depth of water we were in. The odds of finding the harbor seemed poor. Fear and caution suddenly overcame my desire for a quiet berth and giving Oceanside a miss seemed the sensible thing to do. The Bear rounded up quickly as I pushed the tiller down and we headed out to sea on a starboard tack toward San Diego.

The tension eased away and I felt relieved that I had made the right decision.

9 LIFE IN SAN DIEGO

As we sailed from Oceanside toward San Diego, a new course was laid in. beating south through the darkness and fog. I sat in the cockpit giving the old girl some reassuring thoughts after foolishly risking her in the fog off Oceanside. However, she was having none of it. All I felt from her was cold disapproval, somewhat similar to the conditions we were now sailing in. In spite of that, the rest of the night's sail was routine except for a surprise visit from a pair of Dolphins making quite a display of the phosphorescence as they leaped from the water. Most of my time that night was spent in the shelter of the companionway, updating our progress every hour or so, as we continued our way south across the chart, along the penciled course line.

About mid morning, Point Loma slowly became visible as a small blip under the high fog far off to the south. It had been slow going, sailing this coast in the light winds. "Be patient," I thought. I was anxious to get ashore and away from this constant day and night sailing which was becoming so demoralizing. So for the remainder of the morning I busied myself with chores. By two o'clock, Point Loma was off the port beam. Tacking to starboard, we headed into San Diego Bay, bucking an easterly wind. Passing an outbound yacht, still some distance off, one of its crew stood up in the cockpit and pointed excitedly at the Bear. I had no idea what he was saying, but it might have had something to do with the blue insignia of the Bear at the top of the mainsail and the number thirty-five below it. I thought to myself, "He must be a San Francisco Bay sailor. I think we've just been identified."

Not knowing exactly where to go, I headed for Shelter Island and the Police Dock. I had been there once before when working as a professional crew on a large motor yacht, bound through the Panama Canal to Florida. The Police Dock proved to be a good decision. They were very helpful and allowed me to stay the night.

Just as it was getting dark, a parade of yachts all lit up for the Christmas holidays motored by, celebrating the Festival of Lights. For me, this really set the mood for the holiday season. I had given very little thought to Christmas, or anything else except sailing. I was looking forward to taking some time off and enjoying San Diego. This was a milestone for me and I celebrated it that night.

Although I had made many mistakes along the way, I had also been quick to rebound, doing my best, taking on every demand the cruise required. In the past, I had a habit of just sloughing off, but that was not the case now. A quiet voice within said, " Stick with it, don't let fear run you off." This was a new attitude that I hadn't experienced before.

However, I was also very aware of how luck had played such a heavy part in my being here, giving me good reason to doubt my abilities, especially after the Point Arguello incident. After taking a moment for serious thought, I figured it might be a good thing. Perhaps in the future, I would hopefully err more to the side of caution rather than over-confidence.

One thing was for sure, I would have a better chance at success if I just sailed a whole lot smarter. An old mantra came to mind, (Hold what's near, far and what's far, near.)

The following morning I phoned the Harbor Island Marina and secured a berth for a month. I wasn't sure I would need one for that long, but I really had to get some serious rest. Little did I know it at the time, but a pressing obligation to a friend would keep me there for several weeks longer. Pushing off from the police dock was easy enough in the light morning breeze. It was a leisurely sail as I took in the sights along the way to Harbor Island.

Sailing the bay in San Diego was like sailing on a lake compared with San Francisco Bay. It was easy to sail here, and there would be plenty to explore while I caught up on rest. I really didn't have any plans, other than to put a few finishing touches on the Bear before jumping off to Mexico.

Jumping off sounds so permanent, like jumping from a high dive platform into the deep end of the pool. I had to admit to being really apprehensive about sailing into Mexico alone, especially now, because it wasn't much more than a daysail away.

As I remember, Harbor Island was shaped like a sausage that ran parallel to the eastern shore of the bay with a causeway midway from its ends connecting it to the mainland. The yacht harbor was located on the causeway's most sheltered side closest to the shore. As I sailed in toward the harbor there was a side tie that looked vacant. It was an easy landing so

I rounded up and we coasted to a stop right alongside the float. As luck would have it, the harbor master's office was at the top of the ramp.

On the way up to the office I noticed Clarence and Adrian's ketch, Turtle. It would be nice to have some friends here, I thought. The Harbor master was very friendly and most helpful. I told him that I only needed a temporary berth. He went out of his way to find a windward berth when I explained the Bear was engineless. He asked me where I was headed and I answered Cabo San Lucas at the end of the month.

Once settled in, I took a walk to explore the island. It was nice to be here in San Diego. I looked forward to the rest and relaxation I so richly deserved. Besides the yacht harbor, Harbor Island had many hotels and restaurants that were in close proximity to the airport. There were lots of people on the island, mostly travelers on their way to somewhere else. As I explored the island, well thought out walking paths wandered past palm trees and afforded excellent views of the bay, to the north and west.

When I returned, Clarence and Adrian were aboard Turtle. We had a bit of a reunion, comparing our experiences rounding Point Conception. They especially wanted to know how my little boat faired against the infamous "Cape Horn of the Pacific." I gave them the short version about the mighty Bear, and avoided all the stupid parts on my part. But as you know, if the Bear could talk, the story would have been very different. Clarence and Adrian countered with how easy it had been for them motoring around Point Arguello and Conception in a complete calm.

In the days that followed I met other southbound sailors in the harbor. They all sailed Westsail 32's. We had much in common concerning our destination, but not our boats. The other skippers came from the world of big boats which require much more effort to sail, with complicated onboard systems. Consequently, the majority of their time was spent maintaining or repairing all those systems, sailing was a low priority. Not once during our stay in San Diego, did any of those boats sail out to explore the bay or take the time to see San Diego from the water.

The Bear on the other hand went everywhere. We explored the back waters finding derelict harbors, neglected classic yachts, houseboats, and anchor-outs. We also visited the Star of India and other museum boats from the water, as well as beautiful Glorietta Bay that was within sight of the Hotel Del Coronado. Whenever things were slow I went sailing, even if it was only for a couple of hours.

A few of the Westsail skippers decided to team up and replace the batteries in their boats. First, they had to borrow a hand cart and small pickup truck from the local chandlery. They worked together all morning in the hot sun disconnecting and off loading the heavy batteries from each boat. They took the old batteries back to the chandlery and picked up new ones. It was a struggle bringing them down onto the dock before loading them aboard and discovering they wouldn't fit in the brackets that were designed to secured them. By then it was late afternoon and they were really discouraged, knowing the whole process would have to be repeated again the following day.

As I came aboard one of the boats, the guys were sitting around the table drinking cold beers. "Hi guys," I said, "What are you up to?" They told me their sad story, then asked me what I had been doing? "Well, mostly trying to stay cool," I said casually, "But I was really inspired by all your efforts, so I went to the chandlery and bought a new flashlight."

"A flashlight, why?"

"Well, it upgraded my electric lighting by thirty percent."

"You know, that's not funny," one said to the other. "Let's get him. He needs to be dumped into the bay!"

For a moment they both really meant it and were on their feet headed across the cabin to carry out their plan. My eyes got as big as saucers and I promised no more jokes before cooler heads prevailed. After apologizing for being such a smart ass, I was given a cold beer as a reward.

By the third week in the harbor most of us would usually head for a local Mexican restaurant. We would hang out drinking beer and eating chips at the end of the day. Of course the idea was to drink the beer slowly and eat all the chips. It didn't take too long for the servers to catch on to us. They cut off our chips, but it was fun while it lasted.

One evening we were all invited to a birthday party on one of the boats. There must have been ten of us on aboard. There was lots of talk and we were having a good time. The conversation turned to past adventures and a few pictures were brought out. After the pictures had been passed around, our host said, "I have more pictures in the car, I'll get them." We sat there for awhile waiting for him to return. The conversation began to die down. It was getting late and the party began to break up.

As I remember it, I was the first to leave. On my way up to the restroom a person flew by me at a dead run on the walkway. I just got a glance at him. He was out of breath and looked scared. I hadn't seen him in the harbor before and wondered why the rush? The following morning a small group from last night's party were quietly talking over by Clarence's boat. "What's going on?" I said after wandering over.

"Then you haven't heard," Clarence said seriously. "Last night there was a robbery and stabbing in the parking lot at the restaurant on the point."

"Did they catch the guy?"

"That's the problem. The one they arrested was Jim."

"How could that be? He was with us until he went up to get the pictures."

"That's when he got caught," Clarence explained. "He was caught by his car when a witness pointed him out to the police, yelling, "There he is! Get him!" Right after you left, Jim's wife went to find out why he hadn't come back. Going up to the parking lot, she saw the flashing lights and ambulance and then went to investigate. She saw Jim locked in the police car. A bystander filled her in."

"Will he make bail?" I asked.

"I really don't know," Clarence replied, "The family is working on it."

During the next two weeks Jim remained in jail. His wife would visit him so word got back to us about how he was doing. The news was not good. He wasn't eating and the conditions inside the jail were far from satisfactory. Finally, during the third week he was let out on bail.

The tension in the harbor had been steadily increasing. You couldn't help but notice other groups of people quietly talking casting glances our way. They knew the victim, and were sure Jim was the culprit. After awhile, we all became suspect in their eyes. Most of us kept a low profile and went about our business, but with Jim now out on bail tensions increased to the point of confrontation, mostly yelling, making it known that we were no longer welcome in the harbor. However, all but one of us continued to stick it out. We were scheduled to go to court as character witnesses at a Magistrate's Hearing.

My planned time in San Diego had run out two weeks ago. I was really feeling the pressure to keep my commitments, but the hearing was only a few days away and after that I would be free to go. The last few days flew by and before I knew it, we were all filing into the court room for the hearing. The charges were read off. Surprisingly, the district attorney had linked Jim to several other robberies in the area. One, was a convenience store, and the other a gas station. As the court reviewed the facts of the additional robberies, the judge felt there was insufficient evidence and they were thrown out.

Next, we were called to the witness stand one at a time to testify under oath. Questions were asked about Jim's character, how long we had known him, and so forth. When it was my turn I answered all the questions, but just before my dismissal the prosecutor said, "You closely resemble the suspect in appearance yourself. How do we know you aren't the one who committed these robberies?"

Taken aback, I answered as calmly as I could, saying, "I was aboard Jim's boat when the robbery took place. There was also a man running from the scene of the crime, passing me as I made my way up to the harbor restroom. The other witnesses here will testify that I was aboard Jim's boat." As it turned out all the charges against Jim were dropped. When the news got out, friends of the victim were furious with us. With so much tension in the harbor, it was definitely time, as they say, to get out of Dodge.

Before that could happen, the boat had to be provisioned for the trip south. Judy Baum stepped in to help the following day, driving me around until all my errands were completed, even taking me to lunch at Carlos Murphy's. Both she and her husband sailed a Dolphin 24 which they kept in the harbor. Their boat, I thought, was a nice choice for sailing on San Diego Bay. Her efforts on my behalf were very much appreciated. Once the food was stowed under both bunks there was little to do except fill the water tanks.

Water was the thing that worried me the most. The Bear's maximum capacity was only twenty-two gallons. I carefully filled the tank and four canisters, even taking the time to top off the tea kettle. My anxiety had increased to level nine out of a possible ten. Just thinking about sailing down the Mexican coast alone seemed overwhelming. However, the time had come and the lines securing the Bear were reluctantly taken in and we headed out to sea.

10 JUMPING OFF TO MEXICO

I had learned a lot sailing on the ocean and it was not likely I would make the same mistakes again. However, there was something at play with this whole single-handed cruising scenario that I had yet to understand. Consequently, I would once again pay the price for not knowing, placing myself and the Bear in serious jeopardy.

We cleared Point Loma about noon under a grey sky which matched my mood. In spite of that, the fog offshore provided a good sailing breeze. A course was laid in, allowing us to pass west of the Coronado's Islands, well offshore to avoid shipping. The sea was quite lumpy with small waves out of sync with the usual ground swells.

For the first time during the cruise I felt seasick. This was unexpected. I usually don't get sick unless the boat drops right out from under me. I took a pill and climbed into the bunk to think things over. My attitude was not very positive and I felt as though we were sailing into the abyss of no return. To make matters worse, it started raining.

After several hours rest, it occurred to me that the real cause of my seasickness was anxiety. Once I understood what was happening, the sickness went away and my outlook improved. It was dark before I finally got up to make dinner.

After checking my navigation, I found we were making good progress along our course due south. However, the wind had become lighter making life even more uncomfortable in the confused seas. About midnight the chimney from the galley lamp fell into the sink and broke. Fortunately, there were extra chimneys on board. Our estimated position was sixty miles south of San Diego and forty miles west of Punta Banda.

The wind began to build through the night and a reef was tied in about four in the morning. A second reef was put in an hour later, but soon both reefs were taken out as the wind moderated at dawn. During

51

breakfast the wind started to pick up again, but I decided to carry on with full sail for the time being. The Bear was under control and running nicely in patchy fog with the jib winged out, surfing the swells at sevens and eights. It had been a workout running back and forth to the foredeck in the early morning hours. We were now more than fifty-five miles offshore. Our course was changed to a southeasterly one paralleling the coast. By early afternoon there was no traffic to be seen, which made it ideal for reading or getting some much needed sleep.

So what's it like to sail the Bear day after day at sea? Over time, most of what happens on board just becomes routine. Just before daybreak, I routinely find myself in the cockpit waiting for the first sign of light, which will eventually bring the sun's warmth. During the night, the cold and damp creeps into everything, penetrating my clothes with a clammy stickiness. Even after the sun has began it's climb into the sky, that damp uncomfortable feeling remains until about mid-morning.

After blowing out the kerosene lamps, I check the water in the kettle for breakfast. Starting the Optimus stove is always a bit of a challenge. First the pressure control valve on the tank is shut off. Then the hand pump is used to pressurize the tank so the kerosene will flow up into the burner. Next the burner is pre-heated. This is the tricky part. The small cup just above the fuel tank is filled with alcohol to pre-heat the burner and vaporize the kerosene before the stove is lit.

As I sit across from the stove, it swings wildly back and forth on its gimbals. However, it's not really the stove that's moving. The Bear rolls to port and starboard, pitching and yawing as she continues to shoot on the swells, rising and falling in a continual dance.

I manage to fill the small cup on the first attempt without spilling too much of the alcohol. Once the alcohol is lit the flame goes where ever it's been spilled. So there can be more pre-heating going on than was originally intended. It's a good thing there's a pan attached to the bottom of the stove to catch the alcohol, otherwise the bunk cushion would be pre-heating too.

At this point timing is everything. Just before the alcohol burns out, the valve that controls the flame is opened letting the kerosene into the burner. If all goes right and the burner is hot enough, the last of the flaming alcohol ignites the vaporized kerosene creating a blue flame. The kettle is put on.

While the water is heating, breakfast is laid out between my feet on the cabin sole which is a better choice than having it slide off the counter top. The menu is normally instant oatmeal, canned fruit, and coffee. The oatmeal is made thin and the coffee black because there's no milk or sugar.

The instant coffee is always made after breakfast. That way, I only have to manage one cup or bowl at a time. Having coffee is a leisurely time for me, usually spent pondering over the chart estimating how many days it will take to get to Cabo.

The dishes are washed in a bucket filled with sea water. The small amount of hot water remaining in the kettle is used to rinse the salt off the dishes before they're dried with a towel and stowed. With the dishes done, I spend time taking care of myself. Any serious bathing or washing of clothes is normally done in the afternoon when it's warmer.

Only a few other chores remain. The stove and lamps need to be fueled for the coming night. This is done with a small hand pump that was rescued from a junk pile. The pump is plumbed into the Bear's old fuel tank which has about six gallons of kerosene in it. This makes fueling easy. There's a flexible hose long enough to reach from the pump to the stove. The lamps are fueled on the counter top near the pump. All I have to do is remember the exact number of strokes needed when pumping to avoid an overflow. The lamps are then re-assembled and carefully placed back on their gimbals. Just a small bit of kerosene is used to oil the gimbals and keep the lamps swinging free. I never hurry through these daily tasks. It's best to keep busy, but extra time does allow for reading or catching up on sleep.

By noon I'm back on deck watching the Bear sail and enjoying lunch which is usually deviled ham or salami with crackers. After cleaning up, I'll try to catch up on sleep.

As the afternoon grows late the log book is brought up to date. I began to think about the evening meal as something to look forward to. It's the only hot meal of the day, other than the oatmeal. Because the stove only has a single burner, I'm limited to one pot meals which usually result in stews with vegetables and various spices thrown in for taste. As it begins to get dark my spirits flag knowing that another cold damp night is not far off. To lift my spirits, I usually turn on the RDF which is tuned to a popular rock station in Los Angeles. A final on-deck inspection is made of the sails and rigging.

I'm usually finishing the last of the dishes, just about sunset. Climbing back into my heavy foul weather jacket, I'm ready for another attempt at warding off the cold and dampness. There are several coffee breaks taken as needed during the night to keep me alert and warm. All during the day and throughout my routine, I continue to keep a careful watch for shipping, popping up and down through the companionway like a prairie dog. Shipping is an ever present danger. During this time, five ships have passed, three northbound and two headed south. All the traffic is inshore with one exception. As usual, there is no sleep at night other than some accidental catnapping, which always leaves me wondering

"What did I just miss?"

Because the Bear is so low in the water, our horizon is no more than three miles away when we're on top of a swell and I'm standing in the cockpit. It takes less than twenty minutes for a ship on a collision course to cover that distance. This is the reality I must live with twenty-four hours a day. Over time, I have developed an internal warning system using my intuition. Sometimes, from out of nowhere I'll hear, "You had better get up there!" Those words have paid off time after time. Throughout my days at sea, I am always busy and seldom bored.

It's late afternoon and the wind is less than five knots, slowing our speed in the gentle swells. After considerable thought about the trustworthiness of the wind vane, I take in the whisker pole and lower the jib. The spinnaker is set. Our speed immediately improves with the extra sail area. The spinnaker works so well that we carry on through the night without it needing any attention. However, I still worry about traffic because our ability to maneuver is restricted.

The following morning is cloaked with grey clouds spread over a gentle metallic looking sea. We are fifty miles north of Cedros Island. It has become noticeably warmer as we continue south. I detach my lifeline and take the heavy watch coat off, putting it on the bunk down below before returning to the cockpit with a new novel.

Sometime later, after reading about an anchored yacht in Central America whose crew had been murdered at night by a local with a knife. I reflect on what I have just read. Considering my situation, this is not something I should be reading. "Definitely not," I thought, nonchalantly flipping the book over my shoulder.

Shocked by my own actions, I turned to watch the book quickly slide away in the boat's wake. We are moving much faster than I thought and in no time the book is more than a hundred feet away dropping from sight behind the swells. "What if that were a man overboard?" I think.

My attention is quickly diverted to the sound of a rustling sail. The spinnaker has collapsed and is wrapping itself around the jib stay. That had never happened before. I knew it was possible, and I had seen it happen to others and watched them struggle with it. I'm on my feet in a flash and heading for the foredeck realizing the sooner I stop the wrap the easier it will be to fix the problem.

It is in my third step along the port side that I miss the deck and begin my fall overboard. I remember it all so clearly, as it plays out in slow motion.

My left hand slides down the aftermost shroud as I fall.

"Let go of the shroud."

"Cotter keys in the turnbuckles will cut."

"Grab the toe rail, good, got it!"

The warm water presses against my clothes before shooting up my pants legs. Both hands are on the toe rail, but it continues to slide through my fingers.

"Squeeze harder, you're losing it!

Well, at least I haven't lost my hat or sun glasses."

The Bear continues to slide away from me in spite of my best effort. The jib sheet winch passes by as I'm swept aft by the suction of the water.

I grab the winch instinctively with the palm of my left hand and the moving water plasters my body up against the hull.

The slow slide has been stopped.

"Look," I think, "you have two options here. Either you get back in the boat now, or move to the stern, disable the wind vane, and bring the Bear up into the wind to stop the boat.

My instinct says go with plan A first.

However, my first attempt fails, and I am stranded with just my right knee up on deck with the other leg trailing in the water. There are no further hand holds to pull myself aboard. The suction from the moving water is too great, keeping me locked in its grip.

"You've got to do better than this," I think as I slip back into the water.

A mental picture flashes before me, quietly swimming along watching the Bear sail off into the distance as I come to terms with my final struggle.

Still in the water, I figure my second attempt will be my last. I am losing strength, leaving little hope for a third try.

Giving it my all, I haul myself up to where I had been before but still can't make further progress.

Survival kicks in.

Fight!

Forget the fatigue, kick, twist, pull harder!

Slowly, inch by inch, thrashing and kicking I work my way back out of the sea and onto the Bear, tumbling head first into the cockpit.

I stand in a rage, yelling in anger, as though it's someone else's fault. Stomping forward (or sloshing in my case), back up to the foredeck, I yank down hard on the spinnaker and clear the wrap.

With all sail full again, the Bear picks up speed, sailing along completely indifferent as though nothing worthy of mention had happened. Back in the cockpit, I sit down in a puddle of my own stupidity to consider the situation. There is nowhere to go with excuses and blame but to the truth. After attempting every possible evasion, it is still obvious that I am at fault, lacking the mandatory discipline to keep myself safe.

If I am to ever complete this voyage I will have to establish a consistent routine for my own safety. I thought I had, but it is obviously not enough. Could my lack of sleep have something to do with this?

That evening the light wind drops away to nothing. I heave the Bear to and get some very needed sleep. It is still flat calm and very dark when I wake. I can't see the horizon. A billion stars are everywhere, both above and below the boat, as though the Bear is suspended in space. The only sounds that can be heard are those of my own movement and breathing.

The stillness aboard the Bear is interrupted by the feel of a very faint breeze. At first it's just fickle, but then slowly maturing into something we can use. Aboard the Bear, all is quiet, except for a slight rustling sound as she ghosts along in the blackness. Searching for the sound with the flashlight, I find its source and trim in the jib. We sail on for quite some time in complete silence, so deeply quiet that it feels spooky. Only the phosphorescence from the small ripples of our wake give any sense of progress at all.

A feeling of uneasiness comes over me as though something isn't quite right in this deathly silent world. With all my senses heightened, I become conscious of a low moaning sound, almost inhuman, bouncing its faint call off a billion stars overhead. It seemed to be coming from the direction of Cedros and is heard only every now and then. I can't make any sense of it and am curious to know just what it is. It sounds familiar, but I can't quite put my finger on it. Then it clicks. It's a conch shell. I had one aboard my schooner.

Wondering why someone would take the time to blow a conch shell, I think maybe they're just as affected by this night as I. Maybe they're reaching out to others for assurance, sensing their own obscurity within the formidable vastness of the stars overhead.

Throughout the night we feel our way south along the eastern shore of Cedros Island toward its lone village. Seeing no reasonable anchorage there, I head offshore and heave to for the remainder of the night.

After breakfast and a quick review of the chart, we are soon underway. Cedros Village has a rather bedraggled look to it.

As we clear the southern end of Cedros the wind shifts to the south. This really surprises me after sailing hundreds of miles downwind. As we beat into the wind, it continually shifts as I try to make progress through a nasty chop that knocks what little breeze there is from the sails. Ever so slowly, we are being set to leeward down onto Punta Eugenia. I nurse the Bear along as best I can, but in spite of that, it is only a matter of time before we are swept up onto the rocky headland to leeward. Just before it comes to the point of desperation, the wind shifts into the west and increases to ten knots. Quickly, we overcome the current and escape out to sea before turning south again.

Other than the times hove to for sleep, I had been limping along on not more than two and a half hours sleep per day. I was far more fatigued than I realized. So in self-defense, I plotted a course that would take us more than eighty miles offshore to avoid the constant ship traffic. It would be safer out there. Our next planned landfall is two hundred miles to the south.

The increasing winds from the northwest brought gusty rain squalls and large seas as we made our way offshore. At the first light of day, the Bear is sailing with a double reefed main and storm jib in large swells and a dying wind. It had been quite a night. Faced with a wet foredeck and a moonless night, it took a fair amount of courage to change to the storm jib.

It wasn't too long before we were back under full sail again. A ship coming up the coast rapidly closed in on us. As I watched it approach, the ship would drop into the troughs of the large swells, erasing all view of its hull, and leaving just the white bridge of the ship visible as it headed north. As the ship passed, two of the deck officers dressed in whites came out onto the bridge wing to look us over while their ship labored up over the steep swells.

The passing of the turbulent weather brought beautiful sailing conditions and the Bear now carried on day after day with no adjustment to her sheets or course. I took advantage of this fine weather to catch up on my laundry and clean up the boat. Using Lemon Joy, a detergent from the galley, I took a bath in the cockpit with buckets of sea water. The Lemon Joy had a strange effect on my blond hair, turning it almost white over time. The laundry was brought out and washed in a bucket filled with seawater then hung out to dry. After washing, underclothes were rinsed in a small amount of freshwater to avoid skin irritation.

During the heat of the day the Bear was covered with drying clothes as she ran south, wing and wing toward Magdalena Bay. After days of glorious sailing, it all came to a sudden end.

That night it blew hard. To keep the Bear under eight knots, sail was reduced to just a winged out jib on the whisker pole. The main was down and furled with the boom locked in place using the preventer against the main sheet. Earlier that day I had jibed over and we headed in toward our landfall. We were getting close now, so extra care was needed. I expected to pick up the light at Cabo San Lazaro, then work a distance off as we passed by.

Just before going below after the evening inspection, I scanned the deck once more. Stopping midway down the companion way, I realized the jib sheet was not rigged inside the shroud for beating. My usual procedure, when running with the pole up was to lead the jib sheet outside the shroud to avoid chafing. Not feeling like it, I returned to the deck and took the time to lead the sheet properly. Unknown to me, this would make all the difference in the coming hours.

Dinner was made early so everything would be cleared away before dark. Our landfall was expected to be around midnight. The wind and sea remained rough with no letup. Sailing through the night, I kept a steady watch for the light at Cabo San Lazaro. It was hard to see as sea smoke, generated by breaking waves along the coast, cut visibility. At last, there was a light, but I couldn't identify it from the light list. It appeared to be a looming brightness coming from well inland. Going below, I checked the chart again and the distance we had run along it.

Something was wrong, as I pored over the problem. A faint whisper of sound like the roar of a distant crowd crept into my awareness. I resisted it. I didn't want to hear it, but deep down inside I knew what it was. Finally, it forced its way through.

Something was terribly wrong!

"You had better get up there!"

11 UNINTENDED ADVENTURES

My eyes quickly adjusted to a horrifying scene. Surf to leeward on the port beam arced its way forward across the Bear's bow and up the starboard side. "Oh shit, I hate panic! No time for a lifeline. You fall, you die, it's as simple as that. Now move!"

Quickly, the jib sheet to starboard was cast off. Just as I expected, the jib was yanked from the pole by the force of the wind. An instant later the jib was jibed over and sheeted in flat to port. Taking just a second, I played with the idea that we still might be able to sail our way out of this mess with just the jib. But it was no go.

As I moved toward the mast, the sail ties were ripped from the mainsail. Furiously, I hauled on the halyard until my feet came up off the deck before hooking a leg around the mast under the boom to prevent being swept from the deck as the Bear heeled under the new press of sail. The main topped, and the halyard was quickly secured on its cleat. There was no time to coil it.

The Bear, now feeling the full weight of the wind, lay down hard then rounded up as I ran back across the cabin top. A quick glance showed breaking surf no more than several boat lengths to leeward. Vaulting over the dodger I landed in the cockpit. Grabbing the tiller, the last of the lee deck, gently lit through the Bear's ports, disappeared under an avalanche of heavy water tumbling aft. The vang was released.

As the water rushed over me as I sat in the cockpit, the mainsheet was eased and the Bear fought her way back to the surface.

"Come on baby, you can do it," I yelled over the roar of surf.

Sheets of spray shot over the cabin. With water all over the boat, I didn't think we had a chance. I pictured myself standing alongside the battered Bear laying on a deserted beach at low tide. The intensity of the beating wind and the roar of the surf quickly brought me back to the present.

"Just sail the boat," I yelled at myself, blinking salt water from my eyes. The Bear drove hard to windward as I took a quick visual bearing on the surf and the San Lazaro light. The bearing slowly began to change for the better.

We were sailing out of the trap.

As the last of the surf disappeared into the blackness, its roar was slowly overcome by the routine sounds of the Bear at sea. Still, I held my breath. At last, I knew we had escaped. What a relief!

There's nothing worse than having to look other Bear skippers in the eye and tell them you lost your boat when they ask "Back so soon?" I kept an eye on the Sum Log until we were more than five miles off the coast before heaving to on the offshore tack.

The Bear was undamaged. I clipped my life line on and cautiously went forward to retrieve the whisker pole still clipped to the mast and coil the main halyard which was dragging behind the boat. Before returning to the cockpit I stowed the whisker pole then fell on the bunk and slept. I did not sail again until late the following morning.

Before getting under sail, I sat down at the chart table, went through the log book, and over the chart to see where the mistake had been made. It seemed that the light I couldn't identify was in fact, the Cabo San Lazaro light, and I had mistakenly sailed into Bahia Santa Maria. Knowing that, I felt better, but it still didn't answer the question of how all this had come about. That took some sharp thinking from a tired mind, a mind that I had been pushed too hard without adequate rest for much too long.

It was deep fatigue that had distorted my judgment. I had sailed a dead reckoned course for over two hundred miles and relied on it to make a landfall at night. Common sense knows better, especially when learning from experience that the current consistently sets inshore. That was obvious from the many fixes I had worked out in the past, yet this was not taken into account.

Also, I hadn't learned that it takes more than one good night's sleep to make up for weeks of sleep deprived sailing.

If I had failed in judgment, it was my sailing discipline that saved the Bear. I had taken the time earlier to re-sheet the jib inside the shrouds giving the Bear its windward ability. The mainsail was down, but the first reef was still tied in, and it was just the advantage the Bear needed to make her escape.

With that behind us, we headed south for Punta Tosca staying inshore so as not to miss its navigation light. The wind continued to blow and the Bear made good time as she surfed on a blue sea flecked with white caps.

I was still feeling down after yesterday's experience, and my confidence was shot. All I needed to make everything right, was to reach Cabo without any further incidents. That seemed like a realistic goal. After all, what could possibly go wrong with Punta Tosca just ahead? When we arrived in late afternoon a bearing was taken and the light was identified. I knew where we were, but there was something very troubling about the scene.

After Punta Tosca, there was nothing to be seen of the southern coast. It had suddenly disappeared after we had followed it for six hundred miles. I studied the chart, but there wasn't a clue I could find that made any sense of this. Still unable to comprehend the extent of my mental exhaustion, all rational thinking and logic just slipped away like an ebb tide. I was completely beside myself wanting this part of the cruise to be over. I wanted to be in Cabo.

"Maybe this is Cabo," I thought, as I held the coast pilot book open in my hands, unable to comprehend that the Canal de Rehusa and Cabo San Lucas are two different places.

Desperately confused about what I was doing and where I was going, I glanced at the entrance and saw a Grey Whale making its way in toward it. "That's the local knowledge I need," I thought, "I'll follow him in." There were steep cliffs off to port where the last of the coast could be seen diving toward the sea. At their base, was a channel marked in deep blue with white breaking water off to the south. The Bear, reaching across the wind with her lee rail just skimming above the surface, moved in quickly toward the entrance keeping pace with the Grey Whale. I watched the whale intently as it surfaced about a hundred feet ahead, blowing, then submerging for what seemed like forever.

The minutes ticked off.

I began thinking that we were on top of the whale and it would rise up under us. I counted the seconds every time the whale submerged, but it always reappeared right on time just ahead. The channel continued to look good as we passed by the cliffs. There was a small beach under the cliffs with two large white fishing boats anchored bow in. Both crews on board stopped what they were doing and stood in silence watching us as we sailed by. I waved, but not a hand went up in return.

The white tumbling water off to starboard went on as far as I could see with the exception of a fishing boat that had been wrecked in its midst. Turning my attention ahead, I saw the cliffs coming to an end. The water in the channel had now changed to a muddy brown. Opening up before me lay a broad bay with a featureless shoreline that ran off into the hazy distance. It was too open for a sheltered anchorage and Cabo certainly wasn't here. The craziness had finally run its course.

I sensed danger. Tacking, the Bear was brought around to retrace her course. As we began the slow beat back down the channel, the wind had dropped considerably. It was still flooding slightly, making our progress painfully slow over the bottom. "It will be dark before we're able to sail out of here," I thought as the sun slowly sank into the sea taking the wind with it.

Looking ahead, I could still see the two fishing boats anchored about a half mile away. After awhile, they put their anchor lights on, making them visible in the growing darkness, giving me a clue as to where the entrance was. Meanwhile, the Bear danced around in the small confused waves that knocked the wind out of her sails, pushing her closer to the roaring millrace of broken water now barely visible in the darkness. The lead line was cast to check the depth. We were only in nine feet of water. Waves could easily start to break here at anytime once the ebb set in. I put the sculling oar to work. It was tough going with the boat pitching. Slowly, the Bear turned and headed to the other side of the channel. After an exhausting hour and a half at the oar, we reached smoother water and began slowly sailing toward the sea.

Grabbing a snack, I settled into the cockpit preparing for the long tedious sail back toward the open water. An hour or so later, asleep in the darkness, I was awakened to the noise of a large Diesel engine. My head jerked up with eyes wide open. I had no idea how long I had slept, but the Bear was about sixty feet from ramming one of the anchored fishing boats. Reaching off, we easily avoided the collision.

Not a word passed between us and those aboard the fishing boat, but I'm sure the crew was relieved. As we sailed by they shut down their engine. They must have guessed that I was sleeping. Who in their right mind would go to sleep in the Rehusa Channel?

The closer we got to the entrance the more the wind picked up. Finally the Bear heeled to a fresh breeze coming directly off the ocean and sailed clear of the land. I checked the Sum Log and read the mileage. I wanted to be a long way offshore before we hove to again. It was time to stop and think things over after a good sleep.

Slowly waking the following morning, I came to realize that the Bear had been hove to all night and I had slept deeply. The sun was already up flooding the cabin with light. Urgently rushing to the companionway, I quickly scanned the horizon for traffic. All clear. The Bear was lying quietly in ten knots of wind about three miles offshore.

Instead of racing to get underway again, I took my time with breakfast, cleaning up, and setting the boat in order. Only then did I sit down and go over the chart and the courses sailed in the Bear's log book.

I could see nothing wrong with my navigation. After taking another look at the Mexican coast where the land disappeared at Punta Tosca, I considered the problem. Checking the chart after a good night's rest, it was easy to see why there was no land there. The coast turned away to the east. It made sense. Even during the best of times, I had never been a true believer when it came to my own navigation. Still not feeling confident, it seemed to me that a leap of faith was required and I should head south.

The tiller that was lashed to leeward the night before was freed, along with the jib sheeted to windward. The Bear, now awake, surged off downwind with her usual enthusiasm. A distance off was taken from Punta Tosca and a course was laid in for Todos Santos. Soon the whisker pole was set to starboard and the wind vane sailed the boat. By that afternoon, the wind, from the north, was twelve to fifteen knots with a swell coming from the opposite direction. This made me think a distant storm might be responsible for these unusual conditions. By evening the wind had dropped off to about ten knots leaving a sloppy sea. The Bear was jibed over in the darkness, and we began to close with the coast again.

The following day provided very pleasant sailing. Most of it was spent with small jobs about the boat as well as getting myself in order for our arrival at Cabo San Lucas. Just after midnight Cabo appeared off the port beam, as I thought sarcastically, "Well, this would be our arrival time!"

Cabo was beautiful in the moonlight. Both the arch and the beach could be easily seen against the far shore across the bay. Sailing south of the cape, I could see the anchor lights of many yachts in the bay. However, it seemed wisest to sail offshore, heave to, then wait until daylight before going into anchor. Getting a good nights sleep in the calm conditions would make our arrival easier.

Up until now, Mexico had been no more than part of a plan, just an idea, but now Mexico was real. What a joy it was to slide the hatch back, letting the sun in to chase away the night's dampness. Taking my first look at Cabo in daylight from the companionway of my own small yacht was the memory of a lifetime. I had sailed more than fourteen hundred miles to get here. It was such a relief to no longer sail day and night. However, all those miles were filled with adventure, perhaps much more than I had bargained for, but I wouldn't give them up. They were filled with lessons and great experiences.

But for now, emotionally, I was finished with sailing, the whole cruise, everything!

12 PLAYING THE TOURIST

It was early when we sailed into the bay at Cabo and very few people were up. The Bear wandered through the anchorage as a sort of victory lap, allowing me to check out other boats and look for friends. The anchorage was comfortably full with about forty or fifty boats. Most were thirty-five to fifty feet in length. We were not the smallest boat. That honor belonged to a 22 foot Lyle Hess Cutter named Ayii Chihuahua. Turtle was there sailed by Clarence and Adrian along with several of the Westsail 32's from San Diego.

After finding a good spot a comfortable distance from the other boats, the anchor was let go in forty feet of water. The Bear came head to wind, then blew back on the breeze as the anchor reached for the bottom. The chain continued to run out until there was a three to one scope, firmly setting the anchor. The seven pound Bruce was reluctantly set as a stern anchor just to stay in sync with the other boats around us.

After dropping the main and putting in a good harbor furl, my attention turned toward inflating and assembling the dinghy. Soon it was trailing aft on its painter. It wasn't long before the cockpit awning was up to fend off the hot Cabo sun.

A Canadian couple came by in a dinghy to talk. I asked questions about clearing in with the authorities. It was a major concern for me as I had never done it before. They said it was easy enough if the paper work was done correctly and suggested I come in with them tomorrow. They had business with both the Port Captain and Immigration. This took some of the pressure off. The afternoon was spent making sure all the forms were carefully filled out in Spanish with three copies.

Clarence came over in his dinghy to pick me up so I could listen to the morning Net which came on at the same time every day. Anyone could listen in and exchange information. I had read about the Net somewhere, but had no experience with it until now. After the morning roll call, the person running the Net went over old business before discussing new items, such as shopping, restaurants, and if anyone knew how to repair a refrigerator.

Others came forward with advice and possible spare parts, which I thought very generous. Then I became the subject of discussion when someone asked, " Does anyone know the guy in the little boat that just came in? It would be nice to know where he's from." Then the subject shifted to a story about a sudden gale in the northern part of the Sea of Cortez which had decimated a small boat regatta with several lives lost. No one knew anything about it, so it was dropped and the Net was shut down for the day.

Clarence brought me back to the Bear in time for lunch. I asked if he'd like to come aboard, but he declined the offer. After lunch was made, it was taken to the cockpit and shared with a glass of wine over a good book.

The thoughts of the strong gale in the northern end of the Sea of Cortez stayed with me throughout the day, intruding into my thoughts and activities.

It was early when I woke the following morning. The sun wasn't up over the hills, but the sunrise was beautiful with a smear of orange and grey clouds to the east. It was more spectacular than what is normally seen, due to an active volcano in Central America.

Sitting in the cockpit with my morning coffee, my eyes followed the curve of the beach north then westward toward the famous arch which was not visible to me from my location in the anchorage. My eyes shifted to the modern hotels clustered together within the surrounding village hinting the possibility of more change to come. This was confirmed by the modern condos clustered together on a rocky hilltop overlooking the small village. To me, the condos looked out of place in this simple village. I couldn't help wondering what the Mexicans thought of all this. Some of those I spoke to later were not happy with the changes. It was the Americans, they said with mild resentment, that owned the condos and came to the hotels. Their village way of life was being disrupted, which was more important than the money coming into the village. It's natural for some to resist change when it first occurs.

It was almost time to meet with the port captain. I checked again to make sure all my paper work was in order. The Canadian couple came alongside in their dinghy to pick me up. With me in the bow, we headed in for the beach.

The trick to making a good landing was to wait for just the right wave. Ready in the bow with the painter in hand It was my job to jump out when we hit the beach and hold the skiff from being sucked back into the surf. The skipper gunned the outboard and we came riding in on the back of a larger wave. The beach was steep with a quick run off requiring fast work. I jumped out, pulled hard on the skiff's painter, then dug in my heels to keep the dinghy from being dragged back into the surf. We all did our jobs and the dinghy was soon secured high up on the beach. The waves weren't really that big, maybe three feet at the most, but caution was still needed. It's no fun being dumped in the surf.

Before leaving the beach we agreed on a time to meet back at the skiff. We took turns waiting for the port captain and immigration. By watching others, I quickly learned how to work with the officials.

Once inside, I would take my hat off as a show of respect, then stand and wait. My paper work was in order, filled out in Spanish with all forms in triplicate. Thanking them for their time, I used my limited Spanish whenever I could. Once the formalities were over, l was free to come and go.

I made a call home to see if my monthly pay check had arrived. It had. The next errand had me standing in line at the post office. There was a package with a money order and a month's worth of mail. Then off to the bank and finally some money! My monthly budget was four hundred dollars per month. When I left San Diego I was pretty much broke, so it had been a leap of faith to sail on to Cabo, trusting that the money would be waiting. I had Sue to thank for that.

With all my financial needs met, I began exploring the dusty unpaved streets that ran past small adobe houses with thatched roofs. On the way back to the beach, I did my best not to step on any wayward chickens that freely roamed about. As we prepared to get underway, I was assigned to help push the skiff off. The motor started on the first pull and I was back on board in no time. Once again, I thanked the couple for giving me a ride in their skiff which I had earned from hauling it through the surf. It was almost noon before I dried out.

The next few days were spent exploring the village just to get the lay of the land. After surfing onto the beach, the Avon inflatable was dragged up above the high tide mark before being capsized with the oars locked in the boat. During all my time in Mexico the Avon was never bothered by anyone when it was left that way.

Walking has always been a pleasant pastime and I used it to full advantage to locate everything, including the "Washamatica", a small store front with a collection of old coin-operated washing machines. The new pesos I had gotten from the bank were exchanged for American quarters to run the washers. When finished, I took my clothes out back, and hung them up to dry. At first, I thought, "You've got to be kidding, clothes lines!" However, the clothes were dry in about thirty minutes, which was equal to any drier.

Perhaps the most difficult thing to get used to was siesta time. Everything closed from one until four o'clock, the hottest time of the day. So all my errands were usually done in the morning. Boat work was scheduled during the afternoons.

About four days after my arrival, I turned forty. A couple of guys came over from a boat not far from where the Bear was anchored. They borrowed the boots from my wet suit to dive for lobsters. When the boots were returned, each had a lobster inside. I had a birthday invitation from Clarence and Adrian that day, so I brought my two new best friends along and had them for dinner. It was a memorable evening thanks to both Clarence and Adrian.

Several days later, there was a beach party. It was a pot luck affair and everyone was invited. It was a sort of meet and greet kind of a thing. A fellow single-handed sailor struck up a conversation. He was an older retired man with graying hair. When we finished our beers he said, "I have some cold beer out on the boat and would like to talk to you."

"Well, that sounds good to me. What's this all about anyway?

"You'll see," he said quietly, "Meet me at the boat."

I was curious. His boat had been berthed at Harbor Island in San Diego, but I hadn't seen much of him. When I arrived he was in the hospital having his second cataract operation. One of the other Westsail skippers who had sailed down the coast with him said he couldn't see well enough to sail safely.

After following him in my Avon, I came alongside his Westsail 32. I stowed my oars and hopped aboard after securing the Avon. "I'll get you a cold one," he said, as I sat down in the cockpit.

"Here's a cold beer," the skipper said.

"Thanks," I replied. The conversation continued pretty much as it had on the beach for awhile, until he stopped for a moment to casually scan the anchorage. I was quite relaxed in the warmth of the late afternoon sun, and had forgotten about our talk. "I need to talk to you about something," he said nervously.

"Yes, what is it?"

"I have a question about sailing. How do you set the sails?"

"Well, pretty much like everyone else I suppose."

"No, I mean if the wind is coming in toward the side of the boat where are the sails supposed to be?" I was about to take a sip of beer when my mouth fell open in amazement, spilling the beer.

"Are you serious?" I said almost bursting out laughing. I could see that his expression hadn't changed. He was serious! "You're serious, aren't you," I said, quickly regaining my composure.

"Yes. I need help," he said looking away embarrassed.

"Ok, you know the boat won't sail directly into the wind don't you?"

"Yes."

"Then here's how it works. The sails are trimmed all the way in when you sail close to the wind. When the wind is on the side the sails are halfway out. And when the wind comes from behind you let them all the way out. If they luff, trim them in."

"What does "luff" mean?"

"That's when the sails flap. I don't mean to change the subject, but where are you going from here?"

"I plan to sail to New Orleans to visit with my grandchildren." I sat for a long moment in silent contemplation about his chances, before he spoke again. "Oh, thanks, you've been a really big help. You won't say anything about this to anyone, will you?"

"Not a word." And I meant it too. As I thought about it later, I took his meaning to be not telling the others who were cruising with us. As I climbed down into my dinghy, I glanced at the name on the stern of his boat. Lucky Duck, it said. I hoped so.

While out shopping, I met a character from the inner harbor. In a very offhand manner he asked if I wanted to motor out under the arch in his dinghy. "You must be kidding," I said. "Sounds dangerous to me."

"No, it's quite all right, I do it all the time." We got into his skiff which was about nine feet long. Once across the bay we turned toward the towering arch above. Just as we came to its entrance, it filled with breaking water. Heading into it, we plunged up over the waves and through the arch. We were a bit wet, but the water was warm. It was a memorable experience and I have often thought about that time whenever seeing pictures of the arch at Cabo San Lucas.

On my morning shopping rounds, I happened to pass by an open cafe serving coffee near the inner harbor. I had never come this way before. Apparently it was a hangout for Americans and many were wearing the proper yachting fashions. One group of patrons off to the side were complaining loudly about how they'd been mistreated by the Mexican officials. Considering their attitudes, it wasn't hard to figure out why. Not being familiar with their circumstances, I kept my distance. My own experiences led me to enjoy my time in Mexico, finding the Mexican people to be friendly and helpful. In fact, I felt safer in Mexico than in my own country.

One evening the skipper of a small ketch called over to me as I sat in the Bear's cockpit. "Would you like to come over for a drink and dinner?" "When?" I yelled back.

"How about now?"

"Should I bring anything?"

"Only if you don't like gin."

I climbed into the dinghy and rowed over. The skipper took my line as I came aboard. We introduced ourselves in the cockpit of his very attractive Mariner 32 ketch. Soon Don and I were deep in conversation about cruising. He and his wife, Linda, had sailed down from Southern California and were taking time off from their jobs before starting a family.

They had arrived in Cabo about a week after I did. His wife was not aboard at the moment having returned to L.A. on business. I was glad he had asked me over. We went below and he started to make dinner. The boat had a dinette layout with a long counter on one side. He gave me a second drink and started cooking . "Just jam yourself in the corner, it's the most comfortable place on the boat," he joked.

It had been quite rough in the anchorage for the past several days, with swells out of the south. Before going below, I had glanced over at the Bear surprised at how much she was rolling.

The skipper was doing a good job in the galley, but it was one hand for the cooking and the other for yourself. I couldn't help but notice his drink skate along the counter top out of reach, before reversing its course on the way into the sink, only to be intercepted as Don grabbed it. Of course, I didn't know it then, but we would later cross paths several times in the Sea of Cortez. It was a pleasant evening and we had enjoyed each other's company.

Once back on the Bear, I thought about the evening aboard the ketch. It was the standing headroom that made everything so difficult in the rough anchorage. I found it much more comfortable aboard the Bear. Everything was accessible from where I sat. I didn't have to hold on when sitting, so I always had two hands free to manage the galley. Of course, putting your pants on in four and a half feet of headroom was another matter until you learned how to do it.

The following day, the wind and swells steadily increased from the south. We were completely exposed to the open sea. In these conditions I felt it was mandatory to stay aboard. As we bucked into the waves, spray started to drift in through the open ports forward.

It was time to take action. After closing the ports, the awning was stowed, and the Bear was made ready for sea. The dinghy was brought up to the boat and the oars were removed. The excess anchor line for the stern anchor was stowed in the Avon, after securing a bite of it to the Avon's bow. If we needed to leave quickly, the Avon would be anchored and we could return for it later. Next, the anchor line was unfastened in the forepeak. Its end was then tied to a float left up on the foredeck. Now I could slip both bow and stern anchor lines if it got much rougher, and sail to safety. The halyard was connected to the mainsail. I took the sail ties off and pulled in the first reef before furling the sail again. All was ready to quickly get underway if need be. However, the wind peaked within the hour before calming back down. It left a beautiful sunset in jagged clouds, just in time for a pre-dinner cocktail. Of course all of that preparedness could have been easier with a trustworthy engine, that is, if you can trust them.

I have this thing with engines. When using an engine in a sailboat I am always fearful. How long will the engine continue to run before it quits? It's just a matter of time to my way of thinking. This issue however is not really a matter of trusting engines, but can I fix them? Nine out of ten times I can't. Of course, I could learn to fix them if I applied myself. However, learning how to fix engines is not sailing, and sailing is what I do. Therefore, a line was drawn. I've had engines in boats before, but nothing like the one in the schooner, it lived back under the companionway ladder in a box, Pandora's Box, as I came to call it. It was a stranger on board, something like a distant suicidal uncle. With its gravity fuel system, from the Model T Ford era, it would mysteriously fill the bilge with gasoline when I least expected it. It happened one day as we were returning to the berth with a family of four onboard. Thank goodness for good sailing skills, is all I can say about that!

In the calm days that followed, I spent time going for walks just attempting to sort out some of the problems that had driven me to make this cruise. While walking back to the dinghy along the water's edge, I happen to glance up toward the dunes where two couples were sitting looking at the sea. The women were topless as they sat with their men in the sun. At first, the ladies were momentarily taken aback by my presence, then they returned fierce stares, but it wasn't their expression that said you shouldn't be looking. It was an attitude that said, we're in Mexico and we can do whatever we want!

After many weeks of rest and recreation my attitude had improved and I began to think about sailing into the Sea of Cortez. La Paz beckoned and I was curious to see it.

13 THE HORN OF BAJA

As the Net came on, we turned our attention toward the radio located over Clarence's nav station. There was lots of chatter concerning the weather between Cabo and La Paz. No one liked it.

Winds out of the north at thirty-five knots with six foot seas sounded pretty challenging. Most skippers thought they'd wait a few weeks before heading north, or anchor during the day and motor at night. As the transmission ended, both Clarence and Adrian, who knew of my plans, gave me a concerned look but said nothing.

After weeks of relaxation, the demands of the cruise had returned with a vengeance, falling heavily on my shoulders. My only relief would be to see this cruise through. I had a schedule to keep, but unlike most other skippers, I could only sail when there was wind. Without wind there was only the sculling oar to rely on. These were the rules I had set for myself to test the merits of a more spiritual life chosen years before. Now it was up to me to see it through.

There was a friend in the Sausalito Yacht Harbor who sailed his Folkboat to Cabo, but after several attempts couldn't reach La Paz because of the high winds. He sold his boat in Cabo blaming his poor sails. But I thought there was more to it than that. His story became one more daunting unknown that I would have to face.

I was restless and determined to leave which overruled the weather report. This was so like me. I had heard the weather report, but I wanted to see it and feel it for myself. Then I would know I had done my best. My final checks were done before the day was over and I would sail the following day.

To boost myself up I decided on a party. Still having a small amount of bourbon left, I rowed over to a very fancy sport fishing boat with my only pot from the galley to ask the skipper standing two decks above me if they had any ice. This whole scenario reminded me of a scene from a novel in English literature, "Please sir, may I have some more?" Surprised by the request, they gave me all I needed, plus more, saying they were glad I had asked. The ice had been spilling out of the machine for lack of use. It had been so long since I had any ice it was a real treat. Once back on board, I ramped up the music and let the party begin.

Slowly, the anchorage at Cabo disappeared aft into the haze brought on by sullen broken clouds overhead. I had no reality of what lie ahead other than a nasty weather report. So far, the following breeze, contrary to the mood of the day, gave us nice push toward Los Frailes, our next planned anchorage. Things were looking up.

It had been quite a fire drill getting underway, having the beach so close at hand within the crowded anchorage. But having Barbara Jones at the helm helped, allowing me to focus on stowing the anchor and clearing the foredeck.

Barbara was from Sausalito and had sailed south aboard a Westsail thirty-two to Harbor Island in San Diego. That was where we first met. She had been interested in Bears for some time and asked to do a short sail with me the day I left for La Paz. After a pleasant sail around the anchorage, I dropped her off near Clarence's boat, so she could return his dinghy. We didn't connect until I was back on San Francisco Bay when she began crewing for me. She moved on to other Bears before becoming a permanent crew on Bear 34, Joe Bombera's boat. A year or so later, Joe came up to me at the yacht club. Grabbing my right hand in both of his he started pumping it enthusiastically saying, "Dave, I'm so grateful to you for what you've done!"

" But Joe, I haven't done anything."

" You recommended Barbara sail on other Bears!"

" When Barbara started sailing with us, she hit it off with my son and they're now married and have a daughter. I can't tell you how happy I am. I've always wanted a grandchild!"

Of all the boats in the anchorage at Cabo, the Bear was the first to leave for La Paz. Now a fair wind was pushing us toward Los Frailes and we were making good time. I remarked on it out loud, then regretted it immediately. It was bad luck to talk about the wind. Not even a whisper. Soon the seas began to lay down and the wind died.

As I remember, there was a lighthouse onshore. I used it to measure our progress for the next three hours as we rolled and tossed with slatting sails in the confusion of the remaining waves. We slowly sailed by the lighthouse after carefully selecting the most promising cats' paws, only to be abandoned by them a short time later and then drift back sideways in the opposing current. This frustrated me no end, and I guess it would anyone. That's the main reason why so many sailors have engines. But even in this situation, there is a way to make the wind come back. Ducking below, I returned with the scull oar. Slowly moving its blade back and forth in the usual figure eight pattern, the Bear returned to her course. Any forward motion we made with the oar increased the velocity of wind in her sails. Aeolus, the god of wind, seemed to realize we were in earnest and finally gave us passage. The cats' paws disappeared, replaced with the hint of a steady breeze. I continued to coax the Bear along in the last of the twilight.

It was a busy night with lots of wind shifts, but twelve hours later we had sailed twelve miles. As dawn broke, the Bear was hove to in a complete calm with its skipper asleep. An hour later a steady breeze woke me to the hum of wind in the rigging. The wind's call was quickly answered and by mid-morning the anchor was down at Frailes.

The water that had been dark blue on the Pacific side of the Baja peninsula was now aqua. The cove we were anchored in was very attractive with its white pristine beach and good holding ground. Bright green sea grass on the ridges of the sand dunes danced in the steady breeze as we lay head to wind. I was done in and chose to nap on and off for the remainder of the day. It had been a thorough workout the night before with as many as ten changes of wind direction every hour.

Such conditions reminded me of books I had read about sailing through the Horse Latitudes, a zone of intermittent winds and calms. After all, it did seem as though I was sailing out of one wind system on the Pacific side and into a very different one in the Sea of Cortez. What this new wind system had to offer the engineless Bear was a good question. I had no real idea yet and it was too early to tell. However, it was something to think about, and I had plenty of time for that, as the cove at Frailes was deserted with no distractions.

The following morning, I took my time getting underway. When the anchor was secured and everything in its place, we were ready. It had been blowing all night and it was blowing now. Once out of the cove the sails were hardened in and like yesterday, we continued our dance to windward in about twenty knots of wind.

The Bear made good work of it. It was just like being back on San Francisco Bay except the waves were considerably larger and closer together. A larger boat might have had more difficulty due to her length in these steep close waves. Even so, the Bear met the challenge gracefully with spray rattling on the cabin top and streaming off the mainsail overhead as I lay in my bunk reading.

At Punta Arena we tacked over to port. It was one thirty, more than time for lunch, which I grabbed after plotting the new course. The wind dropped to not much more than five knots making sailing in the leftover waves difficult. However, the wind continuing through the late afternoon encouraged me to carry on into the coming night. A short time later it dropped off to nothing in the dark, leaving us to drift on the tide.

A little after midnight, a light breeze filled in from the south-west, then shifted into the east for several hours before coming from dead ahead. These changing conditions continued for several more hours until finally steadying up during a nice sunrise.

After tacking, we sailed on a starboard tack in fifteen knots of wind and headed west toward the distant Baja shore. The wind continued to build throughout the morning and into the afternoon. A reef was taken as the wind increased from twenty-five to over thirty knots.

The Bear slugged on through the box car shaped waves occasionally putting the foredeck underwater when unable to crest them.

The duct tape that was used in Monterey as a hasty repair was no longer holding. Water was streaming in through the fore hatch and mast collar again. It was time to bail. Six buckets later the bilge was clear.

Looking off into the distance Bahia Los Muertos, our destination, was just visible. "Slug on little Bear," I thought to myself. "Slug on, We're going to make it." Instantly, I ducked under the dodger as a big one came aboard swamping the foredeck before crashing onto the cabin top and slopping up over the dodger. The Bear, like the prize fighter she was, shook it off.

An hour later, we entered the anchorage which was unsheltered from the wind by its low lying foreshore, but gave good protection against the waves. Finding a vacant spot with no other boats directly to windward, I watched a large powerboat drag backwards out of the anchorage. She was the second one in the last ten minutes to drag.

Going forward, the jib was hauled down and secured. The Bear was brought head to wind. Once she developed sternway the anchor was lowered and the chain eased out. Because of the thirty plus knot winds, I gave her a four to one scope. The Bear blew off downwind until her bow suddenly swung to windward as she reached the end of her scope. "Good old anchor," I thought, "Never a worry about her."

14 WIND AND WATER

A tight furl was put in the mainsail so it wouldn't escape in the wind. The boom and tiller were also locked in place to avoid any unnecessary movement. I leaned down under the dodger to get out of the wind. Ducking my head below, I took a moment to listen to the boat for the slapping of halyards or anything else that would have to be taken care of on deck before going below. All was quiet except for the swish of water along the hull and the ever constant screeching of the wind in the rigging.

Next, I re-checked our position in the anchorage as a matter of habit using the surrounding landmarks, but already knew the anchor would hold throughout the coming night. We were secure. Down below, I scanned the anchorage from under the protection of the dodger.

It was a dreary place shadowed in grey by a discouraging sky. The beach was littered with kelp and flotsam cast upon it from past storms. As I visually followed the shore's arc to the right, a prominent rock in the vague shape of a skull marked the farthest limit of the anchorage. Beyond that was the wind-whipped sea.

We were secure. It was time to let go. Pulling the jug out of its locker I put it between my feet to hold it in place out of habit, then reached for a wine glass in the galley. Pouring a tall one before sitting on the galley counter in the companionway, I peered out through the salt splattered dodger windows at the bleak scene. "There goes another one," I thought. This time it was a ketch off to starboard dragging through the anchorage.

With the wine finished, I crashed on the starboard bunk. Hours later, waking suddenly out of a deep sleep, I jumped to the companionway to quickly scan for traffic before realizing we were anchored. Nothing had changed. I lit the cabin lamps in the twilight and got a bite to eat before returning to the comfort of the bunk.

After a solid night's sleep, I sat up peering through the port lights, still feeling fatigued. Nothing had changed much but the sun's effort to break through the broken clouds. "Well, at least the sun makes it somewhat better," I thought.

With breakfast over, I turned to sealing the leaks on the foredeck. While working, I thought about sailing on to La Paz, but was interrupted by an older unkempt man who had come alongside unnoticed in a battered dinghy. He told me that a few boats in the anchorage would be sailing north tomorrow and wondered if I might be one of them. After giving it some thought, I said I would.

The wind was still blowing hard with no letup and was likely to do the same tomorrow. I never looked forward to sailing in these conditions, especially when it came to leaving early in the morning. I thought it better for my own morale to sail in the company of others. It would be a nice change.

Lately, I'd been thinking about the Bear, especially since yesterday's sail, and questioned how much more could she take. Anything that broke would have to be fixed by me. What worried me most was that I couldn't fix everything, like a mast for instance.

Major Tillman, a Blue Water medal winner, was in my thoughts. He had managed to sail several engineless nineteenth century pilot cutters successfully into the highest northern and southern latitudes in a quest for mountains to climb. Somehow, he instinctively knew just how far to push his boats without damaging them. Perhaps his success came from just taking the time to listen to his boat. It was worth a try. After all, the nearest boatyard was far beyond my reach.

That night after supper I had a little going away party. Tuning into a Los Angeles rock station, I attempted to lift my mood. My current outlook was not much better than the grey sky I had been living under for the past few days. The wind's continuous screeching was having its way with me. It was depressing. Tomorrow would prove to be an interesting day, but I certainly wasn't looking forward to it.

After a difficult night's sleep I got up early and made breakfast. It was another grey day much like yesterday. The wind had eased a bit, which gave some comfort. By the time breakfast was finished, several other boats were getting underway. With all secure down below I gained the deck to raise the main. It took some extra effort to get the anchor up. The heavy winds had set it well. The Bear was hauled right up over her anchor before the choppy water broke it out.

With everything cleared away, we sailed across the anchorage and rounded the headland of the skull, sheeting in and facing off with the boxcar-like seas again. The Bear handled it well, her stem just clearing the wave tops by inches with the lee rail occasionally awash. As the skull slipped by, about half a dozen people were up on top of it, waving and yelling to cheer the boats on. It was encouraging, but later I thought they secretly wanted to know just how a small boat would fare in these conditions before trying it themselves.

Being the smallest, we were watched the closest. Acting casual, I stood in the cockpit and waved back. Just then, the Bear missed a step and fell into a hole. She failed to clear the top of the next wave which buried the foredeck sending broken water onto the cabin top. That got a rise out of our audience, but unfazed we carried on in true Bear boat fashion.

The further we sailed from the skull, the better the wind became. Finally the sailing conditions were excellent. With that, I left the Bear to the wind vane. This allowed me to get on with the morning chores. However, as time went by the wind became shifty, with headers and lifts forcing me to keep a continuous watch on our course throughout the day. It had been a long day's sail, but as the sun set we had covered half the distance from Los Muertos to La Paz. Shortly after that, the wind stopped completely. Fortunately the seas had calmed somewhat, but we were still left rolling about with slamming sails.

Finally, I took the mainsail down and left the jib sheeted in flat to dampen the roll. I tried reading in the bunk for awhile, but had to brace myself to keep from being dumped out. Giving up, I took my frustrations out on the scull oar, which is a wonderful tool for that. We made very little progress, but it was good exercise and I felt better for it.

About ten that night the wind returned, first as light zephyrs, then slowly steadied up. I took the helm, working the wind shifts to advantage covering another ten miles to windward before giving up and heaving the Bear to, just as a three quarter moon set.

When I woke, it was already light with the sun just above the horizon. Dashing to the companion way, I quickly scanned the horizon. There was no traffic. However, we were less than three hundred feet from Isla Cerralvo and rapidly being set down on it by the flood tide. There was a nice breeze, but it was chilly and there was no time to put on the heavy watch jacket. The jib and tiller were quickly freed and we began sailing into the clear. Soon Isla Cerralvo was behind us.

I went below, dousing the cabin lamps, and began breakfast still shivering from being on deck. Over coffee, I thought about what just happened. Was it blind luck that woke me before we were swept into Cerralvo Island, or had I developed some kind of seventh sense that kept me safe while sleeping? It was some of both, I thought. But it was best not to rely on it. I had always reacted to those subtle feelings in the past and it had paid off.

Checking the chart, we were making good progress on the flood tide and by noon we were five miles from La Paz. The sailing was beautiful with the wind behind us. As the day warmed, I enjoyed every moment. An hour and a half later the anchor was splashed. After putting the Bear to bed, I settled down to lunch with a glass of vino to celebrate and begin the process of unwinding.

Taking in the view, the La Paz waterfront was mostly sandy beach on the south side of the bay. Its northern side was fringed with mangroves, and most of the larger yachts were anchored on the north side of the main channel that ran east-west along the city's waterfront. It was too shallow for most of the cruising boats to anchor close to the waterfront where we were. The Bear was about two hundred feet from the dinghy dock and right in front of the Hotel Arcos, directly across the street from the beach. There were several wharves to the west of us, one which served the boat yard, and the other was used by Mexican Navy.

We had successfully sailed one hundred sixty miles from Cabo to La Paz through some pretty challenging stuff and it was a relief to be here. It was not difficult to understand after our experience why other small boats had failed to reach La Paz. But the Bear made the sail in style regardless of her leaks.

Safely anchored in La Paz, I couldn't help but wonder, would we have these same sailing conditions all the way up the Sea of Cortez? I hoped not!

15 THE BIG CITY

Cars and trucks rushed along the busy boulevard not far from where we were anchored. The hum of traffic, even heard from down below, gave me the feeling of being late for an appointment I didn't have.

Actually, I did have an appointment, but it wasn't time related, just mandatory. Both the Port Captain and Immigration authorities demanded my appearance immediately upon coming ashore. After breakfast, the paperwork for the authorities was filled out and placed on top of the navigation table along with my passport, health, and tourista cards.

Going topside, the Avon was pulled from its box and inflated. Once ashore with the paperwork in my back pack, a fellow sailor on the dinghy dock gave me directions to the Port Captain's office. As I recall, it was just across the street. The Port Captain was, a short man dressed in khakis, slightly unshaven with a bushy mustache, looking perfect for a part in a south-of-the-border movie. He gave me a quick clearance, then sent me off to immigration several blocks across town. A little before noon, I was back aboard the Bear having met all the legal requirements and was now free to explore the city.

While fixing lunch, I looked at the thermometer in the cabin. It was seventy-seven degrees, quite pleasant, making me think of all those cold miserable sailing days it took to get here. It was only early April, but I had sailed into summer. The rest of the day was spent working around the boat, polishing brass, filling lamps and inventorying food and water. The last time I had taken on water was in San Diego. Now there was very little remaining of the original twenty-two gallons.

Where would one find clean drinkable water in Mexico? That was a question I had no answer for. However, the following day I returned from a walk ashore and noticed someone filling a canister from a faucet on the beach. After asking about the water, I was told that everyone used this faucet and no one ever complained about it.

Over the next few days I kept my eye on that faucet as several others used it. Some of the people had big boats and would arrive with half a dozen five gallon cans then work for hours ferrying water back out to their boats. A few days later, I headed for the faucet, filled my four canisters, and returned to the Bear.

The caps were removed from each canister and filled with bleach then poured back into the canisters. With the caps replaced, each canister was shaken until the bleach was well mixed with the water before pouring it into the tank. The whole process was repeated one more time to complete the job. I still had some fears about the water being safe. I could taste the bleach in the water, but it was drinkable. After sampling the water, I waited to see how it would affect me. The last thing I needed was to get sick. The Bear's plumbing couldn't handle that kind of catastrophe. As it turned out, the water was good. It just tasted weird, but that was something I could live with. So I made my coffee a bit stronger and that seemed to help.

Every morning before noon I would go ashore and do some shopping. Not that I needed to get food every day, but more for something to do than just walk around. Often, I would buy tortillas or go to the Mexican bakery. It was fun to watch the baking process which was done outdoors in wood- fired clay ovens.

The Mercado, or grocery, was another place of interest. Often more than half the shelves were empty, leaving me to wonder what had been on them. I was never quite able get over those empty shelves. It was something you never see in the States, and that led to some anxiety about getting what I needed. When something was needed, experience showed it was best to buy it then, because it probably wouldn't be there tomorrow. None of this seemed to bother the Mexican people. I shopped for items of highest priority first, being limited by what I could carry in my back pack.

In La Paz, there wasn't much rushing about. The people seemed happy, taking the time to help others and were much more relaxed than people in the States. A few nights earlier, on a Saturday night, there was a good example of what I came to call Mexican graciousness.

I was with several people I had met in the anchorage. We were having drinks at the Arcos Hotel on the second floor balcony. The traffic below was moving slowly as drivers cruised the main drag on a Saturday night. Suddenly a pickup truck rear-ended a car in front of the hotel. All the traffic stopped behind the accident, then slowly, with everyone cooperating, the cars begin to move around it. There were no blaring horns, fighting for lanes, or yelling "Are you stupid or something!"

The driver slowly got out of his pickup and casually sauntered over to look at the damaged vehicles. The other driver joined him. They quietly discussed what should be done as other vehicles continued to move past them. It was about that time the driver of the pickup realized he still had an open can of beer in his hand. Slowly, he sauntered back to his truck and stashed the beer behind the seat before returning to talk to the other driver.

Up on the balcony, we Americans found this hilarious. We all knew what would happen if this situation had occurred back in the States. There would be flashing red lights, handcuffs, or a possible fist fight before it was all over. As we continued to discuss the situation, I glanced back down at the scene in the street, but everything had returned to normal. The drivers had sorted out their differences and moved on.

Standing in the cockpit one morning I noticed a panga, which are used as water taxis and work boats, dashing about from boat to boat in the anchorage. As I watched, the panga's skipper was either collecting bags or handing them back to the people aboard their boats. As the panga came near, I waved it down. The skipper told me he was picking up laundry and would be returning it the following morning. Reaching below, I grabbed my bag which was quite full and handed it over, hoping I could trust this fellow. True to his word, he returned with my laundry the following morning neatly folded in the bag. The price was very reasonable.

As a lover of boats, I found the pangas quite curious. Their hull shapes were just the opposite of what you would want when using a big outboard motor. The pangas were long narrow boats with clipper bows and tiny-wine glass shaped transoms. This made them squat badly when they accelerated with their large engines. Even though built of fiberglass, it was easy to see their heritage sprang from the hollowed out log canoes in use a century ago. These pangas were found throughout my travels in the Sea of Cortez.

The longer I stayed in La Paz, the more people I met. Several of them were real characters, but the Frenchman was by far the most interesting. He lived with his companion on a ketch that he had built. The boat revealed much about the man through its construction and choice of color. It stood out in the anchorage. As I remember, the ketch was painted red from the masthead right down to the waterline.

As I rowed by one day, he called out to me with an invitation to come aboard. Once settled in under the comfort of his awning, we introduced ourselves. The skipper was an older man in his sixties. His wife or companion, I'm not sure which, was about his age with greying hair. They were well tanned, physically fit, and curious about me and the little boat I was sailing.

Mostly, his questions were about the mechanics of handling the boat alone, but hers were more along the social line, such as don't you get lonely, or have you met anyone along the way? Answering their questions as best I could, I said, "I was better off sailing alone."

After awhile, the talk turned to his life's adventures and experiences. It quickly became clear the Frenchman was quite worldly and had boundless confidence. As a young man he had traveled to the Amazon River Basin in search of work and adventure. He found work at a logging company that needed wooden tug boats to tow the freshly sawn logs to the mill. Never having built a boat before, he told the mill owner it was not a problem and he'd get right to it. Then he told me in great detail how it was all accomplished.

Occasionally his wife would jump in saying, "Isn't he great, he can do anything!" She had the highest confidence in him. He enthusiastically jumped right back into the conversation, mentioning that he also had built the boat we were sitting on. I complemented him on his workmanship. Being young at heart and still full of adventure, he left me with the feeling that I was capable of living a much larger life. We parted ways after I invited them to come and see the Bear.

A few evenings later, at twilight, I watched the moon slowly rise through the palm trees that framed in the Hotel Arcos. A skipper in a nearby sloop yelled over inviting me for a drink. I rowed over to his boat which was larger than mine, but still under thirty feet. After we exchanged names, he said, "Here, I want to share this with you," handing me a glass with a clear liquid in it.

"What is it?"

" It's what the peons drink, not legal, but easy to get. Taste it." Cautiously I took it a sip. It was strong, way above what I expected and made me think of a similar experience I had in South Korea where a drink had been spilled on the table as we drank at Johnny's Road House. Johnny, who was waiting tables at the time, quickly said, "No problem," pulled out his cigarette lighter and lit the fluid on the table which burst into a blue flame. Anxiously, I momentarily glanced up at the thatched roof overhead, then back down just in time to see the last of the flaming liquid disappear.

Back aboard the skipper's boat, we continued to share our drinks. The skipper explained he taught at a state college and was on a sabbatical leave like myself. However, his story just didn't quite add up from my point of view. His boat told another story. There was thick trailing grass that had grown on the boat's hull and anchor line. The boat hadn't been sailed or cared for in a long time. I think he was just living aboard rusticating, hiding from the demands of life. As it got late, he gave me what remained in the bottle before I returned to the Bear in darkness. The following evening I poured the remainder of the bottle into a glass and chased it with grape fruit juice, but the juice instantly curdled.

During an evening out I had met a young lady at least fifteen years my junior. We got to talking about John Steinbeck's book, "The Log of the Sea of Cortez." She was crewing on a large Nordic trawler yacht down from the L.A. area. They were following Steinbeck's cruise, using his book as a guide. I was aware of the book but hadn't read it. She asked me to come out to the Nordic Trawler for a tour of the boat. Actually, ship was more like it. The vessel was well over sixty feet long with a freeboard so high you almost needed a Jacobs Ladder to get up to the deck. A crow's nest was on its foremast for keeping watch. Everyone aboard seemed to get along well together. When I left she gave me her copy of Steinbeck's book.

I had waited for days before the morning was calm enough to change the topping lift. My four fall tackle was hauled to the top of the mast on the main halyard. The bosun chair was attached to the tackle at deck level. After securing the boom to the top of the dodger the topping lift was removed from the boom.

Once in the bosun's chair, I hauled myself hand over hand up above the spreaders. Securing the chair, I took a break by resting my feet on the spreaders. Waiting for the calm conditions was the right thing to do. With my weight above the spreaders the Bear was acting squirrelly. It's one thing to go up a mast in a berth with the boat tied off four ways, but completely different when at anchor. Hopefully, no pangas would come racing by. After un-belaying the tackle I continued on to the top of the mast. The Bear was very squirrelly at this point, forcing me to wrap my legs around the mast and focus on staying centered. Even with slight movements the Bear would heel several feet from vertical at the masthead.

The topping lift was quickly removed and the ends were switched. I could see there had been wear on the lift where it passed through its cheek block on the mast. Once the opposite end of the topping lift was rove through the cheek block and passed down to deck level, I took a quick look around. The view was excellent. I could see over the anchorage and out to the Sea of Cortez were I would soon be sailing.

Starting down the mast, I noticed a large power boat dragging its anchor, drifting down toward the Bear. By the time I had reached the deck, the Grand Banks 32, was almost upon us. I started yelling until someone came topside. When the problem was explained the skipper began to go forward to start the engine. Calling him back, I told him it was already too late for that. He looked doubtful until I pointed out that his boat was already over my anchor line. "Go forward and pull in on your anchor," I said. A moment later the two boats were clear. The skipper explained that the boat was just a charter, as though that made a difference. I replied there was no damage done. It was best to forgive and forget considering my own mistakes from my not so distant past.

After spending several days reading the 'The Log of the Sea of Cortez', I had progressed to a point where the Western Flyer, the boat Steinbeck had chartered, was in La Paz during Easter. Steinbeck had mentioned the tradition of selling sweet pastries at the door of the church after Easter services. I went to the church as the service was letting out, feeling a connection to Steinbeck, I watched the sweet pastries that were still being sold more than thirty years after he had written about it.

Waking with a feeling of restlessness, I started my day with the usual routine, but it was no good. The weight of responsibility could not be shaken. Two weeks had gone by in what seemed like a moment since I had splashed the anchor in La Paz. It was time to get moving again.

Arrangements had been made before I left San Diego with a trucker to meet me in San Felipe six hundred miles to the north in mid-June. But knowing how engineless sailing goes, I felt it was best to get an early start. Most of the day was spent on last minute issues, before preparing to sail the following day. I had no idea how far we'd get or what we'd face, but I needed to make a start. I had to trust that it would all work out.

As I was busy working in the cockpit that morning, a pop, pop, bang forced me to look up. A Douglas commercial airliner, known as a DC-3, had just taken off when its right engine exploded leaving a trail of black smoke and flame. The plane slowly circled back to the airport and made
an emergency landing.

Just for a moment, I thought this might be an omen of things to come, but pushed it away, thinking the sailing would be challenging enough without any omens getting in the way. I continued on with my tasks. When finished I used the rest of the afternoon to clear for Loretto one hundred and fifty miles to the north. That evening, just as the sun set in a fiery display, a dolphin swam close by the Bear blowing as it went. Perhaps this dolphin was a good omen after all.

I would need all the help I could get concerning good omens. The gale mentioned on the Cabo Net still continued to haunt me. That gale had been sudden and ferocious. It had overwhelmed small boats, and claimed a few lives in the northern Sea of Cortez. I had experienced similar storms and knew the fear and destruction they could bring.

As I sat down below studying the chart, I couldn't help but guess about what could go wrong. Would I have the ability, and courage, to successfully sail the Bear six hundred miles north to San Felipe?

Only time would tell.

16 ENTERING A DIFFERENT WORLD

As the Bear's bow pointed toward open water, I found the Sea of Cortez to be a very strange world. It was not like any place I had ever sailed. The winds change constantly and are just the opposite of what I had experienced in the Pacific. Gone were the days of sailing without a single sail adjustment or course change for the better part of a week.

There was very little wind when we left La Paz. The anchor was wrestled aboard under broken grey clouds. Just as I finished clearing the foredeck my sailing hat went overboard. In the excitement of getting underway, I had forgotten to clip its lanyard to the collar of my shirt.

Jibing around quickly, I ran to the foredeck to retrieve it, but it had sunk beyond my reach, leaving me to watch it slowly disappear into the depths below. That hat was a real loss. Its design was quite rare and difficult to replace.

The light wind made for slow sailing until about a mile beyond the last channel marker when it gave out completely, leaving us stranded dead in the water just off a beach resort filled with vacationers. I envied those people playing in the water, having the freedom to come and go as they pleased. It wasn't long before one swimmer, brave enough to swim the distance, came out to the Bear. He was quite tired, clinging to the rail and asked to come aboard. Resting on the side deck with his feet in the water, we exchanged names and talked for awhile.

He was a student from the local university seeking a college degree, but hadn't decided on a major yet. As a student, he was impressed that I was a teacher. This surprised me. It was the first time in my experience that someone actually gave the teaching profession such sincere respect. Usually, well meaning parents said such things as, "I don't see how you do it, it's hard enough just to raise my own two," which is a nice compliment, but lacks respect for the profession. As a student at a party, I once told the wife of a school superintendent that I planned to go into teaching. There was a long silence as she stared at me incredulously, before saying

"Why?"

My passenger found it difficult to believe that the Bear, or the "little boat" as he called it, had sailed all the way from San Francisco. We talked for awhile longer before wishing each other well. He slipped back into the water and swam for the beach so as not to overstay his welcome.

By now it was late afternoon, but there was still no prospect of wind. My cruising guide showed Ballandra, several miles away, to be the nearest anchorage. Just as I was getting the sculling oar out, Invictus came alongside with Don and Linda aboard. I had met Don earlier when he had invited me for dinner aboard their ketch in Cabo. It was good to see him and finally meet Linda. Don offered me a tow, which was gratefully accepted. I promised them some wine for their efforts.

As the wind came up, they cast me off before motoring on ahead. The sailing was good for awhile, but I was left becalmed on a copper colored sea mirroring a remarkable sunset. Sometime later, after a determined effort at the oar, the anchor was dropped in forty feet of water. The Bear's momentum snubbed against the anchor as we swung to face it.

Don and Linda came aboard after I was settled in, leaving their dinghy trailing behind the Bear on its painter. There wasn't much room in the cockpit so I entertained them from the companionway. I asked them how many other boats had left for La Paz. They said that most were still waiting for better weather. We toasted the cruise and shared our plans. The next stop would be Loretto where we hoped to meet again if I wasn't too slow in getting there. As the stars came out, my guests returned to their boat.

A quick supper was made and the dishes were washed. Bright green sparkles of phosphorescence danced around the dishes as I rinsed them. Once the chores were done, I settled into the cockpit with a cup of coffee to enjoy the evening. It was very dark, but the clouds had cleared and the stars were out in full force. There were billions of them so close together that they appeared as clouds. All was at peace as the Bear sat upon the glassy water.

About two-thirty, I was awakened to the sound of wind humming in the rigging and the Bear pitching in the waves. Sticking my head up above the dodger I saw a completely different scene than the one of just a few hours earlier. Boats once quite distant, were much closer as we faced a new wind from a different direction. The lee shore, an old lava cliff, was less than two hundred feet behind the Bear. Other anchored boats had shifted in close on both sides making an escape under sail difficult should the Bear's anchor start to drag.

It seemed best to formulate a plan. The real problem was the big anchor I had down. It would take extra time to get it up, especially on a pitching foredeck at night. At first, I wanted to jump into action and make my escape. However, it seemed smarter to stay where I was. The risk of hitting another boat or being blown ashore before we could get underway were real possibilities. So I thought it best to give the anchor more scope and hope for the best. After several anxious hours I was able to get some sleep. The anchor continued to hold well, passing the first of several very difficult challenges yet to come.

The following day was really my first introduction to sailing the Sea of Cortez. The anchor was aboard by nine o'clock and the Bear was headed for Espiritu Santo Island some five miles off shore. The chart showed five or six coves as possible anchorages on the island's western side. Sailing slowly along the island's shore, we looked in on each cove. They were all beautiful, just like pictures you would see in a charter boat catalogue.

As the day wore on, the wind became more fickle stranding us from time to time in complete calm. During those periods, I would duck below to get out of the heat and just let the Bear drift.

Grabbing a snack and some water I glanced up at the cabin thermometer. It was one hundred degrees. Hoping this wouldn't be a forerunner of what was to come, I tried to imagine sculling the Bear in this kind of heat, but didn't think it would be possible for any length of time.

By late afternoon, we had just about run out of coves to investigate. The distance to Isla San Jose, the next anchorage, with the current winds was too far to cover under sail before nightfall. And sailing at night was not recommended according to the cruising guide.

The closest logical choice for anchoring was Partida. The guide described it as a drowned volcano. I found this intriguing and thought about how many opportunities I would have in the future to sail around inside a volcano. Just about that time the wind came up, and the Bear was headed into the volcano's west entrance.

Both the north and south facing sides of the crater's walls were close to two hundred feet tall as we passed through the entrance. They were quite rugged, composed of red rock and very steep right down to the water's edge, which is what you would expect when inside a volcano. The east side of the rim, which had been partially destroyed sometime in the distant past, provided a good corridor for the breeze to pass through. A barrier beach of white sand filled the gap in the damaged section of the eastern wall, giving the anchorage good protection from the sea.

One other yacht, a fifty foot ketch, was anchored about one hundred yards off the beach. Sailing by it, I waved to several people onboard. Using the lead line, I sounded my way in until there was twenty feet of crystal clear water under the keel before anchoring the Bear to a white sand bottom. The view was spectacular. The setting sun hung just above the crater's west entrance, enhancing its interior walls with rich red terra cotta colors and contrasting deep blue and purple shadows dramatically defining the crater's overall ruggedness.

After furling sails and securing the Bear for the night, I dropped below and poured a glass of wine before returning to the cockpit. "Ah, so this is how cruising is meant to be," I thought, while leaning back against the boom. It had been a near perfect day.

Moments later, my thoughts were interrupted by the sound of a fast moving skiff coming alongside. Kit and Jerry introduced themselves and handed me an ice cold beer as a welcome to Partida, then invited me to dinner. They were attracted to the Bear and wanted a picture of her. As I attempted to go below, so as not to be in their picture, they asked me to pose for them. Once the pictures were taken, the Bear's drop boards were put in place and we headed back to the ketch.

As I remember, the ketch had a clipper bow with a bowsprit and a traditional taffrail around the stern to balance out the boat's style. The varnish was in good condition and the decks, although somewhat worn, were bleached by the sun and salt giving them a pristine look. The boat's spars were varnished with the halyards thoughtfully tied back from the masts to avoid chafe. The white sail covers matched the white hull. The crew was a happy one and I immediately felt welcome. It was refreshing to have people to talk to. Dinner was served as we all sat around the table or on nearby bunks. Everyone became quiet as they focused on their steak and salad. I couldn't remember when I had eaten so well. After dinner the skipper asked lots of questions about the Bear and what my plans were. He was quite curious about why I would sail such a small boat so far.

While speaking of his own sailing experiences, he suddenly stopped mid-sentence and said, "You're not listening, look at me when I'm talking to you!" At this point, all conversation in the cabin stopped as the crew watched intently.

"Oh, I'm sorry, I said, I must have slipped away. I'm not used to being around people very much. I apologize."

"Not paying attention to your host is a sign of disrespect."

"I meant no disrespect," I said, attempting to ease the situation.

He returned to his story and the crew relaxed. The rest of the evening went smoothly.

Kit offered to take me back to the Bear. As we pulled up alongside he said he would send me a photo. I was relieved to get back, still feeling somewhat chastised over my conflict with the skipper. "Well good luck," he said as he pushed off and returned to the ketch.

Pulling the drop boards and stowing them under the dodger I went below to light the lamps. After returning to the cockpit, I began to mull over the evening aboard the ketch.

Beginning to feel more comfortable in my solitude, I was distracted from my thoughts by a sparkle of light on the water. The night was very dark in the volcano's caldera without the moon. But the sea still sparkled and that made me curious. I had never seen the sea that way before. Taking one of the buckets from the cockpit I scooped up some water for a closer look. With a flashlight, I could see very small animals swimming in the bucket. Bright green concentric rings of phosphorescence radiated outward as I poured the water overboard. When it came to natural beauty, this place was a sailor's paradise.

The following morning I was up early and we were underway by eight o'clock sailing on a southerly wind. Once out of the volcano, the whisker pole was set and we ran north at about five knots. About noon off Isla San Francisco the wind began to die, but the flood tide took up our cause and carried us along the shore leaving Isla San Jose off to starboard.

Slowly the light breeze veered heading us, and at that point the party was over. In these conditions it would be impossible to reach a good anchorage before dark so we were forced to sail on through the night. The unsteady wind kept me busy, constantly tacking and trimming sails. Each time we were forced to change course it was plotted on the chart. Throughout the moonless night, the Bear was at risk with unlit islands and reefs close by. At one point we were sailing four knots racing blindly through the darkness. Our speed created a brilliant wake. Its phosphorescence was so bright that it illuminated the cockpit with the exception of my shadow, and reflected brightly off the after end of the cabin trunk.

Having several unlit islands and reefs close by wouldn't have been a problem on the ocean. You would hear the sound of surf and see the broken water, but not in the Sea of Cortez, where the water is unusually calm. Our situation began to improve when the moon came up at one-thirty. Soon after that, the wind shifted, allowing us to adjust our course away from the danger. Finally at four in the morning the wind gave out completely. The Bear was hove to and I got some much needed sleep until nine-thirty. As I slept during the calm, the Bear lost at least a mile due to the ebbing tide.

The following morning a course was laid in for Bahia San Marte. It was a pleasure to see daylight again after such a difficult night. Isla Santa Cruz was still off to starboard. It was one of the unlit islands that I had worked so hard to avoid during the night.

All that day we sailed through hot listless weather attempting to make up for the lost distance and to reach our destination. Finally the wind increased, and with the last of a favorable tide we were soon anchored at Bahia San Marte.

Tides that had been barely noticeable in Cabo San Lucas were beginning to play a significant role in our progress north. It was my impression that there were two tides every twenty-four hours and as luck would have it, the flood tide ran north throughout the daylight hours. This remained mostly true throughout the voyage.

It had taken two days and the better part of one night to cover the sixty-five miles from Partida to Bahia San Marte.

Sailing at night had yielded very little progress and it felt good to finally have the anchor down. Once anchored, I would often celebrate at the end of a difficult passage. Sailing in the Sea of Cortez under sail and oar was a battle of wits and determination. I wondered if I would ever get a fair wind, but so far, the odds seemed to be against us.

Rolling over on my stomach in my bunk the following morning, I peered out the companionway squinting up with one eye at the red strip of spinnaker cloth tied to the backstay. I felt like a defeated boxer face down on the canvas. If there wasn't any wind, it didn't make sense to get up.

However, the blue telltale was just lifting, wagging lazily in an uncertain breeze, just enough to tease me out of my bunk to start the day. "Well, maybe it will be better out on the open water," I thought, as I struggled to get up. Still tired, I did my best with breakfast. This wake up ritual soon became a morning tradition as we continued to slowly work our way north.

You might think, What's so hard about going sailing everyday? After all, you have the wind vane to do the work. Well, it's not quite that simple. The Bear is moving all the time when not at anchor. There are currents from tides and winds that choose to blow or not. Visibility is both good and bad as day shifts into night. All of these elements constantly change during a twenty-four hour period. Also, there's the constant anxiety of not being able to reach your next anchorage during daylight. This brings an unrelenting tension. You're never relaxed, constantly racing the boat to get the best out of her as you sail. Overtime, it results in chronic fatigue.

Well, you say, why not stop and rest? This is a good choice and is the right thing to do, when needed. But when the Bear is at anchor, the clock still runs. At anchor, resources continue to be consumed, especially water. This forces you to keep moving through a hostile environment with very limited resources.

For now, we are anchored at San Marte sharing the cove with one other boat. The farther we sail north the fewer yachts we see. I hadn't spoken to the other skipper in the cove until just before getting underway. He rowed over to warn me about the shoal at the western edge of the cove.

Once everything was cleared away from breakfast, the anchor came aboard and we began to sail. Checking the course I found the Bear was headed a little too close to the shoal at the corner of the cove. The course was corrected. Being a little lazy, I avoided using the sounding line and opted for just glancing down through the clear water to check the depth. As I looked, the bottom was rapidly shoaling revealing our sideways drift in the current toward the sandbar.

The sculling oar was quickly brought up from down below. Using all my strength the Bear responded as I bent the oar to the task, but the water continued to shoal. "There can't be more than a foot under the keel," I thought. "We're going to hit!"

Desperately, I quickly glanced back down at the bottom as I continued to sculling furiously, but the shoal had disappeared. We were clear. The other skipper yelled over, "I told you."

"Well, luck of the Irish," I thought, but took that back, replacing it with how about trying for the skill of the Irish next time.

Now that the fire drill was over and we were settled in on our course, I gave some thought as to what the coming day might bring, but really didn't have a clue. Each day was different, but in some ways they were all the same. The major events throughout a normal day's sail were a series of light winds, hot temperatures, and lengthy calms. This endless routine was only broken by rare sightings of wildlife, or an occasional panga off on the horizon. It was enough to wear down any enthusiasm I had for cruising. When faced with a new day, my attitude was to roll out and get to work, much like a trucker would when out on the open road. It was only the evenings at anchor that provided any relief from this routine. As usual, the wind got progressively lighter as the day wore on. And by late afternoon it became clear that we wouldn't reach our next anchorage before dark. This left us with the prospect of sailing through another night. As we continued on, we worked with what little wind we had until about midnight when it gave out completely.

The Bear had a rather defeated look about her as she sat in total calm with the stars reflecting upward off the sea. Her jib hung limply backed in the hove to position with her tiller tied to lee, sitting in the deathly silence of our surroundings.

Sometime later, the quiet rustle of sails and a slight heeling of the boat brought me up off the bunk. It was four in the morning. There was wind, but as usual, not much. Moments later we were underway in the darkness, and a short time after that, the invisible island of Monserrate with its hidden reefs and shoals offshore were put behind us. We made steady progress sailing between Danzante and Carman Islands. It was chilly in the early morning breeze, but by nine-thirty it was totally calm again. At this point we weren't far from Escondido which was our intended anchorage. After using the calm to take a break for breakfast I washed out my cereal bowl.

I froze as our eyes locked. Not more than forty feet away a grey whale poked his head above the surface to watch what I was doing.

17 THE SAFE ANCHORAGE

After the whale had finished watching us and the dishes were done we headed for Escondido. It would be a safe anchorage to leave the Bear before proceeding north to Loretto. This was the plan, but first we had to get there. As usual, there was no wind and three miles to go. The sculling oar was brought out.

I took a little time to grease its leather to make the sculling easier. The jib was dropped to the foredeck and the mainsail was winged out with the vang to provide shade. Starting out with long slow sweeps as I had always done, the Bear began to move with a sailor's gait, first rolling a bit to starboard and then to port as she gathered way. As I watched our progress through the water, it made me question just how effective my sculling was. It seemed as though my energy was not very efficient.

As I worked the Bear through the glassy calm, I resisted the effort it would take to correct the problem. Then after some thought, asked myself what I'd have to lose? My first attempts at trying a shorter quicker stroke began to make a noticeable difference. Encouraged, I began to experiment with ways to quickly shift the angle of the blade in a fraction of a second between strokes. Noticing my arms were getting tired, I began to use my legs and body weight to push and pull each stroke. This eased the stress on my arms allowing me to scull longer without rest. An hour later the Bear was moving right along. Why hadn't I thought of this before?

As I continued to practice, other aspects of sculling came to mind. Was I subconsciously tensioning muscles not needed, adding to my fatigue? What about attitude? Sculling should be a meditation, not work. Work is a word used when resisting activity.

"Ah, the zen of the tiny bubbles surfacing from the trailing edge of the blade," I liked the idea of it. Perhaps meditative breathing would also help. Slowly it occurred to me that the sculling was becoming easier. I was on the right path. Later, I wrote to Tony about it in a letter which went something like this: (Dear Tony, Now I know why I put larger cockpit drains in the foot well. They serve to carry off the sweat brought on by sculling for hours on end. The mainsail only serves to provide shade. I scull through more intense heat than I thought possible, continuing to push and pull that demon oar as the pearly bubbles lazily rise in the cool water from the trailing edge of the blade. Down here, wind is a true gift when you can find it! Best regards, Dave)

After two hours at the oar I was still excited about how much I had learned in such a short time. A light breeze began to fill in. Somewhat reluctantly I stowed the oar on deck. Funny thing about that oar, every time I used it the wind came up. This time it was a light reaching breeze. Perfect!

Courageously, and not knowing what we were facing, we entered Escondido, the first small lagoon, under mainsail only. Just beyond that was a narrow channel, not much more than a gully about fifty feet wide that led into a larger lagoon surrounded by mangroves. At this point the fisherman on the beach stopped mending their nets and stood watching. Yachts don't sail into the lagoon at Escondido. They knew why, but I didn't. About two thirds of the way into the gully the wind shifted dead ahead.

The oar was at the ready. Sculling furiously, I fought to keep the Bear's momentum going as the mainsail luffed lazily in the breeze. At first, it looked like a losing battle. There was no room to tack so I just kept going with the oar. Finally, after a desperate struggle, the Bear just cleared the last of the gully by a fraction before falling away onto a port tack and sailing gracefully into Laguna Escondido. It was an accomplishment to sail into the lagoon. After all, anyone could have motored in.

When it came to sailing, I found that just conforming to what everyone else did was not acceptable. My sailing style has always been considered by others as controversial.

After finding a nice spot some distance from the other anchored boats the Bear's big bronze anchor was splashed and we settled in for the duration of the day. It had taken twenty-nine hours to cover the last thirty-three miles. None of it was easy.

From the look of this place, it was worth all the effort it took to get here. Off to the west, less than a mile away, jagged mountain peaks rose to five thousand feet above the lagoon's surface, colored in a variety of reddish terra cotta shades. Deep within the recesses of the mountain's shadows, random grays and purples reinforced the ruggedness of the steep mountain walls.

In the 'Log of the Sea of Cortez', John Steinbeck had visited here in the Western Flyer to harvest invertebrates from the edges of this lagoon.

The lagoon was impressive. Most of my afternoon was spent in the cockpit periodically taking in the view, as I continued to read Steinbeck's book. Dan and Linda came in on Invictus later that evening and rowed over with a bottle of wine. We talked and made plans to hitchhike into Loretto the following day.

Loretto had been the headquarters for the California mission system. It consisted of a string of missions built by the Spanish that ran north from San Diego to just beyond San Francisco. This was an important part of my travel study project for the school district.

Dan came over and picked me up the following day in his dinghy. Walking out to the road, we were soon picked up by a Mexican in a canary yellow Volkswagen Beetle. With the radio blaring Mexican music and the windows down, off we went at full throttle. It was quite an adventure as I watched the little white crosses flash by along the roadside. I hoped we'd get there soon. The driver was ok with that and he couldn't get there fast enough. However, I was concerned about our arriving in one piece, but wasn't quite so sure the driver knew how important that was to us.

Perhaps I should have complained, but an old saying came to mind. Beggars can't be choosers. It was with my great relief when we arrived. Perhaps he had read my mind after all. Down here in Mexico it was the "Vaya Con Dios" spirit that oversaw all travel.

We split up after arriving, going our own ways, promising to meet at a designated point and time. After mailing letters and calling home, I cleared in and out of Loretto to save the time of making a second trip.

Most of Loretto had a desperate air about it. Only a few streets were paved. Other than the church, the architecture appeared quite minimal in design, but very practical in use. It seemed clear that the hot dry climate was the real architect here. There was very little vegetation in the town, implying a lack of water which I assumed limited its growth and development.

We were fortunate in being saved from the stifling heat by a nice breeze that had worked itself into a twenty knot wind, making us anxious to return to our boats.

Standing at the edge of the road it wasn't long before a friendly driver in an old Datsun pickup stopped and offered us a ride. Quickly jumping in the back, I expected our return to be just as fast and reckless as our first ride, but much to my relief that was not to be. We arrived safely, but somewhat windblown from riding in the back of the truck.

The wind, which had now decided to out do itself, had increased to over thirty knots. As we looked out on the troubled anchorage heavy with whitecaps, another sloop had dragged down on Invictus and the two of them were locked in destructive combat. Don and I, quickly took to the oars and rowed out to the boats as warm spray blew over the bow of the dinghy. It was hard dangerous work to separate the boats and re-anchor the wayward sloop. Don went back in the dinghy and picked up Linda. Don was really upset about the damage which probably amounted to several thousand dollars in boatyard parlance. But what he really couldn't understand, was that no one in the anchorage had come forward to help when we weren't there.

I was very anxious for the Bear's safety as the conditions steadily worsened, but accepted Don and Linda's invitation to dinner. They needed some sympathy and whatever consolation I could give.

It was quite dark when Don offered to take me back to the Bear. I hadn't rigged an anchor light and was concerned about finding her in the darkness, but by now our way was well lit by lightning which had developed all across the western sky during dinner. With both of us rowing in the high winds, we found the Bear right where I had left her.

As soon as the cabin lights were lit, more scope was let out for the anchor and a leather was fastened to the anchor line for protection against chafe at the bow roller. The standby anchor, a Bruce, was also brought to the foredeck for instant use if needed. Everything that could be done was done. Now it was just a case of monitoring the situation throughout the night. Several times during that wild night, as the lightning flickered brightly throughout the cabin, my thoughts drifted back to the day I bought the big bronze anchor, now holding us so securely to the bottom.

"You're not going to take that anchor with you," Pete said, "It's too big," just kept pushing into my thoughts. I couldn't help but smile as the wind screamed through the rigging while the Bear pranced in the angry waves throughout the flashing lightning and booming thunder.

The following morning it was flat calm when I went forward to haul the anchor, but it wouldn't break free. Dan saw me struggling with it and came over to help. You'd think he had enough problems without worrying about me, but that was the kind of person he was. After the anchor was up, I attempted to sail out the entrance on a very light breeze, but the tide was already flooding and quickly flushed us out of the gully backwards. After sailing about I was invited to side tie to Invictus and wait for the tide to change.

Finally, Garrett Smith, who was also anchored at Escondido, pulled me out through the channel with his Boston Whaler later that morning.

At first there was little breeze outside the lagoon, but it slowly developed into a good sailing wind. By one-thirty we were off Loretto and making good time with the help of the tide on our way north.

The wind increased. A reef was put in while the Bear continued to slug her way through short steep seas for the next four hours. The Boat's quick motion made me worry about sea sickness, but it went no farther than that.

The Sea of Cortez is famous for its short steep waves and as good as the Bear was, she failed to climb over some of them giving herself a thorough bath before we reached Isla Coronados.

The following morning, as I was having breakfast in the cockpit, small black birds looking like miniature coots, about the size of those familiar little yellow Rubber Ducky's seen in toy stores, began to pop to the surface all around the boat. Soon there were a hundred or more of them floating all around us just as though we weren't there. Then, suddenly, one would dive to be followed in close sequence by all the others. They repeated this aquatic ballet again and again, until quite mysteriously, they failed to rise to the surface and were never seen again.

At the first sign of a new breeze, the anchor came aboard and the Bear settled easily into her daily routine, but it didn't last long. Sailing in light airs, we made about five miles north, but lost ground in seven hours of calm forcing us to sail on through the night. This time; however, our night sailing was a real money maker. A light breeze developed from the south and we made good progress against an ebb tide. That breeze died just before midnight, but I was able to scull over to Punta Pulpito, visible in the moonlight. Once anchored, we were secure from losing ground to the ebb which ran out for the remainder of the night. It had been an exhausting day.

The farther we sailed north up the Sea of Cortez, the more I begin to feel an increasing sense of loneliness. After anchoring and spending a brief time on deck, the sense of isolation would drive me below to the familiar comfort of the cabin. John Steinbeck also commented on his own sense of isolation by flatly stating in his book, "There is no one here." Sometimes, weeks would go by before seeing another person, and even then, it would be a fishing boat way off on the horizon.

After dinner I would use the radio direction finder to search for new radio stations. This became a hobby when I wasn't listening to rock music from Los Angles. My search for distant stations reached as far as Tennessee. To keep busy, I also spent time adding up my daily mileage and used the cruising guide to scout ahead for future anchorages.

After two days of waiting at Pulpito, a breeze finally came up that I took at a moment's notice. The wind veered aft becoming a mild southerly and the Bear ran north with the spinnaker up. Off in the distance, a Columbia 30 was also headed north. It was the first yacht I had seen in a month, and on sighting it, yelled out, "Sail ho!" The sighting turned into an impromptu race which ended at Lino Bay where we came to anchor.

Jim and Judy, aboard Far Out, were from Ventura. They came over in their skiff and asked if I wanted to join them for a walk on the beach. I was happy to get off the boat after weeks aboard and brought a bucket to hunt for shells.

The beach was steep and consisted mainly of pebbles. Back some distance from the water was a high natural barrier that had been shaped by big waves in the past. Lino Bay was more of a roadstead than a sheltered anchorage. The conditions here were too rough for sand to maintain a foothold on the beach. This was not a place to be anchored when the weather went bad. I took a picture of the Bear at anchor. Viewing this picture later, I was struck by the desolation and emptiness of the surroundings. However, it had been a nice day and I had managed to meet some new friends and get a nice collection of shells, many which were completely unfamiliar.

The following day I left Lino Bay about a half hour after Jim and Judy, but later passed them having more wind farther offshore. The plan was to stop at Domingo Point, but I decided to sail on to Mulege.

Mulege is the only place along the Baja shore where a river flows into the Sea of Cortez. It's marked by a lighthouse on a large rock at the entrance to the river. As we approached under a grey overcast sky, I could see some tall masts reaching up from behind the lighthouse. This encouraged me to sail into the river. My large chart didn't show the depth of water there, but those tall masts behind the lighthouse implied boats over thirty feet were anchored in the river. With the wind behind us, entering the river would be risky. Still, I thought it was worth a try. So with the jib down, and all ready, we headed in. I began swinging the sounding line about a hundred yards out from the entrance feeling no bottom. As we got closer the bottom began to shoal at the entrance and then held steady.

By now I could see the boats in the river were trimarans, probably drawing not much more than four feet at best. However, we continued on into the river. Quickly, the Bear was spun into the wind and the anchor was dropped. We had three feet of water under the keel. I knew we'd ground out in the mud at low tide, but didn't see it as much of a problem because we were quite sheltered.

Being anchored in the small lagoon at the river's mouth was different than anywhere else I had been in Baja. My first impression reminded me of a lake in San Francisco's Golden Gate Park.

The river's shoreline was covered with a mixture of trees and palms that looked similar to lush jungle. If a couple of alligators had cruised by I wouldn't have been surprised. As I looked past the two abandoned trimarans, the river narrowed and made a broad curve off to the left toward town about a mile away. Later that evening, I checked my cruising guide and found the river was often used as a filming location for Hollywood movies in the thirties and forties.

The following morning, the sky was still grey. It had been that way for days. Fortunately it would keep the temperature down as I walked into town. The dinghy was assembled. As I pushed off, I noticed the Bear was on the mud, heeled slightly at low tide.

Before striking off down the road the dinghy was hidden behind a bush. Once I arrived in the village, it took some doing to find the port captain who lived up in the hills surrounding the small village. I cleared in and out at the same time, saving a trip. Once my official business was completed, I began to explore the village. There were not many people about and few shops were of interest. The only point of interest to me was the church, which was built of stone. It was more elaborate than most of the churches I had seen. Other than the church, the village had no distinguishing features about it other than its thick foliage, thanks to the river.

I walked over to the beach to look at the pangas and watch the fishermen mend nets. Offshore, the water was unsettled and restless, somewhat like my mood.

Mulege was very quiet. It was a good place to ditch your worldwide fame for a while. As I remember, the town had no paved roads and very little traffic with one exception. Some Americans were towing a Nordic twenty-seven on a trailer that had broken down. They were attempting to fix it with limited success. I had no idea where they were going and they looked too busy to be bothered with my questions. So, I just slipped by them unnoticed and took a side road out of town.

The road climbed over several hills covered with brush and small trees broken by open grassland. Passing a penitentiary in a valley below, I continued on a short distance before re-tracing my steps back to the boat. As I returned along the road, I couldn't help but notice a small house. Unlike many of the others I had seen in Mexico, it was built of wood and painted green with red trim. It had a thatched roof, somewhat ragged around the edges and a front porch. The dirt walkway leading up to the house was lined with broken chunks of concrete painted white. A leaning palm tree shaded the house's front porch on sunny days and made a convenient place to hang one end of a comfortable hammock. This little place struck me as so much more attractive than the glaring white condos clinging to the steep hillsides above Cabo San Lucas. But that's just me, I always prefer a little of the offbeat.

That night it began to rain lightly with lightning flashing over the mountains to the west. As the first drops splattered down onto the cabin top I began to worry about flash flooding, thinking maybe we should get out of the river, but then thought about the high winds and the lightning at Escondido. Besides, it was almost dark and probably not a good idea to leave. Soon the rain stopped, but just the same, I stayed up late and read.

I had planned to leave the following morning, but it was not possible. The Bear was aground, but the tide was flooding so it was just a matter of time before the Bear would float. The dinghy was stowed and the boat was made ready to sail. A gentle breeze was blowing into the lagoon off the restless sea, which made beating out through the narrow river entrance difficult. As I awaited the tide, all kinds of scenarios rushed through my head about sailing back out of the river, most with bad endings. I often did this when sailing out of tight place. However, I usually got through without a hitch.

Prior to this I had sailed a twenty-five foot sloop for six years without an engine throughout San Francisco Bay and its delta with no problems. There were occasional groundings at times, but I was always able to rescue myself.

The tide was now at its peak. The main was hauled up and the Bear was brought up over its anchor. Then with a heave, the anchor was quickly rolled aboard.

During what seemed like a brief moment, the Bear took the opportunity to wander over to the far shore determined to put herself in the bushes. I cut her off. Steering out of the river, the main was eased a little to pick up speed in the fair wind. As we neared the big rock with the lighthouse on it, the wind suddenly came from directly ahead. The oar was quickly put to use to keep our momentum up. It was tough sculling as the stern pitched up and down in the choppy water, but I kept at it until we were clear of the big rock and lighthouse that had blocked the wind.

As I remember, it was late in the day and we didn't sail very far before anchoring again for the coming night. It was a rough night and we were exposed to a lot of rolling and pitching. The sun in my eyes woke me. It had been almost a week since I had seen the sun. After a leisurely breakfast, we got underway, sailing against the remainder of a slight ebb in four knots of wind. There was a light swell from the northwest which was unusual. Our sailing conditions were about as good as could be expected in the circumstances and we made steady progress toward Punta Santa Inez.

Just as we arrived a small twin engine plane buzzed the resort on the point twice before landing out of sight. We sailed in under the lee of the point, finding good holding ground and quiet water. The view was so pleasant that I decided to stay for the rest of the day.

So far the cruise had gone smoothly with the exception of good winds. However, I was beginning to have my suspicions about the possibility of trouble headed our way. I could just sense it.

18 SANTA ROSALIA

The Borrego Del Oro Resort was the first sign I had seen of anything resembling a modern culture since leaving La Paz. Not realizing how much I had missed that, I sat in the cockpit lost in thought, looking at the resort on the bluff above with its red tiled roofs, white walls, and well manicured gardens.

As I sat quietly in the warmth of the sun, there was more. The Sea of Cortez was changing. It was subtle, but a sixth sense warned me there was danger out there. I looked out beyond shoreline as a capricious breeze scuffed the water forming random cats paws that played on the water's surface. The sea didn't look dangerous at all, inviting us to come forth and frolic.

The weather to the north; however, was not as predictable as it once had been in La Paz. Storms were moving in with little warning as I continued sailing north. They brought up old memories of the storm reported on the Net back at Cabo San Lucas. No one had given much credence to that storm at the time. But I remember how it affected Clarence and Adrian when they heard the report, then sat in silence looking at me, avoiding the obvious question, are you sure you want to go there? How could a small boat regatta be decimated by a storm from out of nowhere? It did seem more like fiction than fact, but never the less it continued to haunt me. And because of that, I wasn't about to easily pass it off. Tides that were hardly noticeable in Cabo, were now much more significant.

Stepping below, I sat down at the nav table and opened the cruising guide to search for information. A moment later there it was. Spring tides could be as high as sixteen feet. Sitting there, I thought about the real challenges such tides could bring with their faster currents opposing any efforts I made to sail against them, especially with the consistently light winds we had been having. Even on a good day, we seldom ever sailed more than three knots for very long.

To make matters worse, the guide also foretold of fewer anchorages. This would mean more exposure to open water and increased night passages in rapidly changing weather conditions. Even the water was beginning to change. It was losing its clarity as we sailed closer to the Colorado River Delta. This meant I wouldn't see a shallow bottom before grounding on it. All of this added up to increasing risk as we sailed into the northern end of the Sea of Cortez. No wonder there were so few yachts this far north.

The following day we got an early start and headed out toward Punta Chivato. Once underway, I settled in on my bunk for some reading. Occasionally, I'd check for traffic but mostly depended on my hearing. Other than the few yachts I had met along the way, the Sea of Cortez was completely empty.

As we neared to Punta Chivato, I saw Far Out anchored in its lee. Jim rowed out to say hello. I hove the Bear to and we talked of future plans. He told me someone had asked about the Bear over the Net, wondering where she was, and if I was alright. No doubt, Jim had filled them in.

Then he asked if I knew Dan and Linda on Invictus. "I first met them at Cabo," I said. It was then that Jim told me their story. They were headed back to San Diego when they were hit by a ship and dismasted. Fortunately, no one was hurt and their ketch, Invictus, survived badly damaged. They were now back at Cabo making repairs.

Jim said he planned to stop at Santa Rosalia, so I said I'd see him there. It was a slow struggle to sail around Punta Chivato, but once it was behind us, a delightful southerly breeze filled in and pushed us along at six knots with the spinnaker up. The breeze finally began to give out in the late afternoon. The Bear was forced to beat along the western shore of Isla San Marcos in light head winds. In those conditions we were just able to eke out an anchorage on a shallow shelf exposed to all winds just before sunset as the tide turned against us.

I couldn't help but envy Jim and Judy as Far Out motored by, headed toward Santa Rosalia. My anchorage was a real worry, but it remained quiet all night as the tide ran out. Later in conversation, I asked Jim why he didn't anchor with me that afternoon at San Marcos. He said it was too exposed. He was right and I wouldn't have stopped there either If I'd had an engine.

Isla San Marcos was larger than most of the uninhabited islands we had sailed by. It was surrounded by high cliffs with a gypsum quarry located on the upper part of the island that could be easily seen from a great distance off. Other than fishing, it was the first sign of any industry I had seen since leaving La Paz.

The following morning was beautiful for sailing with high scattered clouds and a ten knot breeze from the north which made for an easy reach into Santa Rosalia. It's always fun to sail toward your destination in a fair wind, as you impatiently watch it grow in size, revealing unseen surprises. The Bear made such good time that we arrived early, a rare thing for us.

Santa Rosalia was the terminus for the ferry that connected Baja with the mainland. It had a well-developed harbor with a concrete breakwater. As we sailed into the harbor, there was a large light blue cutter anchored near Far Out in the northwest corner of the basin, well out of the way of commercial traffic. I took this as a hint and anchored a short distance from the cutter.

It wasn't long before I met Tom, Arleen, and their two daughters. Their cutter was named Ly Kou. She was built in Vietnam of teak in the nineteen thirties then sailed by way of the Mediterranean to the United States. Tom explained that she was a sister ship to Anahita that was successfully sailed around the world in 1936 by Louis Bernicot.

I asked Arleen how the girls were being educated. She said they used correspondence courses from Calvert, commonly used by cruising families. The girls seemed well-adjusted to life aboard the cutter which I found surprising, only being familiar with kids their age in school. Tom said their girls had never lived anywhere else. I asked the girls if they would rather live in a house, but after giving it a moment's thought, they didn't like the idea very much. So off they went, up to the foredeck to play on their swings that hung from a lowered twin staysail pole that was normally used for sailing in the trade winds.

Tom offered to show me the boat. She was a real classic that had seen very little modification over the years. The galley was aft on the starboard side with two settees forward, separated by a drop leaf table. Forward of the mast was the toilet, or head in sailors jargon, nestled between the two forward vee berths. There were no bulkheads in the cabin, so the entire interior of the boat could be easily seen once you stepped below. This simple layout was typical for many boats built during that time period.

It was comfortable to be anchored in a secure harbor again. Directly to windward was a cement plant that put out toxic dust from its tall stacks. Every morning I had to wash down the boat starting with the cockpit before I even dared step into it. The fine dust was easily spread. A boat yard was just off to the left of the cement plant where two large wooden fishing boats were under construction.

Once my boat chores were completed the following morning, I checked in with the port captain and immigration before touring the town. Santa Rosalia's architecture was completely different from any of the other Mexican towns I had visited. Historically, it was a company town constructed by the French for the workers who labored in the mines. The majority of buildings were built of wood, many of them with second stories and front facing verandas. The streets and sidewalks were paved and busy with pedestrians during the cooler hours of the day. There was even a clock tower up on the highest hill that could be easily seen by everyone. Shops, each with their own speciality, lined many of the streets. Trees were quite common throughout the town adding greatly to its appearance.

After some exploring, I found a barber shop. It had been months since I had been in one. It was a bit of a struggle to get my ideas across, but we came to an agreement and I was happy with the haircut I got.

Sometime later, I found a general store that had everything any person might want, and sure enough, up on a high shelf, there was something for me. The clerk got the ladder out and brought it down. Covered in dust were three blue stackable enameled pots with a carrying handle. The handle was not really necessary, because I figured the Bear would do the carrying for me.

Those small pots fit nicely in my sea swing stove. Now I could stack and rotate the pots to cook three things at once with my single burner stove. After some experimentation that night, I found it worked well, much more civilized than throwing everything into a single pot.

Tom came over in his skiff the following day and talked about the Sea of Cortez and where he had been. He had already been to San Felipe and told me about the new harbor that had been built a short time ago. I looked it up in my guide, but there was no mention of a new harbor. Tom drew me a map of the harbor from memory on the back of an old chart and brought it by the following day. I thanked him for it.

When I bought my cruising guide everything appeared to be up to date, but of course this was based on my assumption that nothing ever changes in Mexico. At least the guide was more contemporary than my chart of the Sea of Cortez, first drawn in the eighteen seventies.

Tom was a good source of information for everything I needed including water. The following day Tom and his family met me ashore. He had two empty five-gallon plastic jugs and was wearing his sea harness. I asked him what the harness was for, but he just said, "You'll see." After a long walk to the far side of town, we filled our canisters from a pipe sticking out of a hill owned by the water company. Tom strapped the jugs to each side of the bottom of his harness giving him the advantage of using his shoulders and hips to support them. All he had to do was guide the canisters with his hands making them much easier to carry.

He had less trouble carrying his ten gallons for the mile and a half back to the boats than I had with my five. By the time we returned, my knuckles were about to drag on the ground.

The most interesting sight in Santa Rosalia was the church of prefabricated iron. It had been brought around Cape Horn in a sailing ship from France. It was designed by Eiffel, the man responsible for the tower in Paris. Standing there in the heat looking at it, I couldn't help but wonder how hot it must be inside that church. My stay at Santa Rosalia had been longer than expected, but there was still much to see.

Cinco de Mayo was coming up, so I decided to extend my stay. The whole town took part in the celebration which started with a parade. Everyone was in traditional dress. The children danced to traditional music, followed by military marching drills. The marching was interesting. All the commands were given with a bugle. It was later explained by a bystander, that voice commands couldn't be heard during parades or in a military action.

After my extended stay in Santa Rosalia, the old anxieties that had been pushing me from the beginning now forced me to move on. I had a date to meet a trucker in mid-June at San Felipe and I didn't want to be late. All this had been predicated on a phone call I had made in San Diego months before. The driver was to meet me with his trailer and haul the Bear back to San Diego. How we were going to get the boat on the trailer, I had no idea, as there were no haul-out facilities in San Felipe that I knew of. All I knew was that the hauler had done this before, but only with power boats. This plan seemed more like a wish and a prayer, making me anxious every time I thought about it.

There were other options, one was to sail the sixteen hundred miles back through some very unpleasant water during the hurricane season to San Diego before school started. The final option, an unthinkable one, was to sell or abandon the Bear.

The sea was flat with winds at two knots out of the south when we left Santa Rosalia. Getting the anchor up was a major job. It was caked with thick black mud that refused to be washed off with buckets of water. After placing the anchor in its chocks the mud was scraped off and dumped overboard by the handful. When finished, both the Bear and I needed a serious wash down. Deeply stained, the bronze anchor never looked the same again.

Around lunchtime, the breeze filled in nicely, veering toward the west and increasing throughout the afternoon to twenty knots. The Bear had a good bath beating through the rough conditions before the water smoothed out toward evening, leaving a gentle swell and light wind from the northwest.

About ten that night we were sailing on the wind in complete silence when suddenly there was a loud whoosh off to starboard. To say that it was startling was an understatement. I was on my feet in an instant before realizing what it was. Nothing could be seen in the total blackness, but It was my guess that a very big whale was close at hand.

Still standing, and very concerned, I tried to penetrate the darkness searching for it. Then ahead in the blackness off to starboard, phosphorescence appeared in the shape of a large green worm more than twice the length of the Bear slowly crossing our course ahead. Still standing gripping the dodger, I stood transfixed waiting to see what would happen next. Slowly, the Bear ghosted through the last of the phosphorescent trail, and the danger was over.

The next day the Bear lay anchored at San Francisquito. It was dark before dinner was finished. The dishes were washed in the bucket, then left on the counter to drain before drying. I took the bucket to the cockpit and emptied the water from it.

The water in the bucket flashed bright green as it hit the sea. This phosphorescence wasn't even close to normal. It was remarkable! I scooped up another bucket and peered into it with a flashlight. The plankton in the bucket were much thicker than those seen earlier at Partida. Throwing a full bucket of water up the side deck, I watched as the deck instantly flashed bright green before the water flowed down through the scuppers, cascading into the sea as miniature green waterfalls. Bright concentric rings radiated outward from the waterfalls contrasting sharply with the dark sea.

The bucket was filled again, this time I fanned the water into the air over the sea. The instant it left the bucket the water turned bright green with the intensity of a fireworks display, hitting the water with spectacular results. The next hour was spent throwing water everywhere before reluctantly turning in. Nothing I had ever seen compared to this, not even the fire fall at Yosemite National Park.

However, there was one exception, that unforgettable moment up at Coeur d' Alene, with the northern lights pulsing overhead on mirrored waters with my young bride in the canoe, drifting among the lily pads. Several days later, while reading my cruising guide it mentioned the phosphorescence I had experienced, and told of the explorer, Cortez, who had also mentioned it in his log.

The next several days brought continued light winds, but some exciting moments and serious concern for the Bear's safety.

19 GET OUT IF YOU CAN!

It all happened so suddenly. The Bear quietly glided to windward through still water, and I was deeply focused on writing up the log. Heavy splashes broke the silence, as though someone was struggling in the water. I rushed quickly topside to see a large stingray jump out of the water and land on its back. Others were starting to do the same all around the boat. These were big fish, most had six foot spans, with some larger than that. As we sailed along, their numbers continued to increase, until there were fifty or sixty jumping all around us.

The closest ones would sometimes land on their backs no more than ten feet from the Bear, which I thought was much too close for comfort. I kept waiting for the inevitable collision, picturing a ray upside down in the cockpit with its tail thrashing about, pinning me in the bottom of the footwell. But as it was, the Bear just continued to slowly amble through the breaching rays untouched, like someone searching for a dance partner. In the late afternoon the rays disappeared as quickly as they had come.

That evening as I was rinsing out the dishes, one of the rays came up to visit. He was curious, with a strange looking mouth much like the intake of a jet fighter. He watched me from less than six feet below the surface before slowly backing away and returning to the deep.

The following day the giant rays returned about mid morning and continued their jumping until late afternoon before disappearing. Although they were interesting to watch, I was relieved when they left.

The following morning it was the usual drill, rolling over in the bunk and checking the blue streamer for wind. Pathetically, it was barely lifting. The evening before, I had looked in the guide to see what lay ahead, hoping for something more encouraging. Bad news however, we were about to enter the Salsipuedes Canal. The guide translated Salsipudes to mean, "Get out if you can." That gave me real pause. "After all I've gone through, and now this," I thought! Can it get any worse?

Thinking back to the kind of ships the explorers used, the translation of Salsipudes began to make sense to me. Considering the technology those early explorers had, it would be difficult for them to make much headway in the conditions we had now. A mental picture formed of them towing their ship with a long boat. The Bear could easily outsail one of those ancient caravels in these quiet conditions. "Well, there's really no choice," I thought, "I've got to give it a try." This was just one more challenge to be overcome. Soon the anchor was up and we sailed into the Salsipuedes

The wind was light, as usual, from the northwest with a slight swell. It remained steady as we struggled to windward in very hot weather. The heat was so great it distorted the shapes of distant islands into shimmering mirages. One island took the shape of a blacksmith's anvil while another stood on its head.

I stayed in the cockpit all day well aware that we were being pushed hard by the flood tide, sometimes through sharp rip currents that created overfalls slopping aboard and knocking what little breeze we had from the sails. The current was moving us faster over the bottom than we were able to sail, so it became necessary to keep the Bear's course clear of islands and reefs well ahead of time to avoid being swept into them. By mid afternoon the wind had disappeared, stranding us off Punta de las Animas.

We had come more than fifteen miles but were now dead in the water. The tide was about to turn. Grabbing the oar, the Bear was sculled toward shore. It was time to get an anchor down before we lost what we had gained from the flood tide. This was not a place to be floating about with no wind in the middle of the night. With the jib down, the mainsail was run out with the vang to provide shade. The Bear slowly headed in, looking for an anchorage. Even under the shade of the mainsail it was very hot work.

Taking a moment to wipe the sweat from my brow, I looked up at the clouds. They were in the shape of mare's tails which reminded me of the rhyme, "Mare's tails, tall ships carry low sails."

"Wind would be nice. I wish it would blow," I thought, as the oar continued its tick tock pendulum swing as the blade flashed from one stroke to the next.

Of course, if there were someone else on board, maybe they would have had the sense to say "Be careful what you wish for" when they took their turn at the oar. But that was not our reality. As the time went by,

I used the motion of the oar in an easy meditation, composing another letter to Tony.

An hour later the Bear came into twenty feet of water and the anchor was let go close to a hostile looking piece of shoreline with nothing to offer but trouble. Its only advantage was the shallow water it offered to hold the anchored Bear against the ebbing tide.

I was completely beat and wanted to sleep but knew that anytime conditions changed, we'd have to leave at a moments notice.

Having slept soundly through the night, the morning ritual of the blue telltale was forestalled as I was cast about on my bunk at daybreak. Taking a quick look topside showed why the Bear was unhappy. The water was way down with sharp currents generating small waves swirling about the Bear's hull. It was shocking to see rocks shaped like pillars some five or six feet above the murky water where there had been none when I had anchored at the top of the tide. The water had lost its clarity making it impossible to see more than a couple of feet below the surface.

Obviously, these conditions demanded more caution when anchoring now that the tides were over ten feet. Should anything happen, there would be no outside help and few resources found in an empty desert that quickly became steep rugged mountains.

During breakfast, the light wind started to pick up, a good sign I thought. Soon the anchor was aboard and we were underway sailing the last of the Salsipuedes in a good breeze. That wasn't so bad," I thought as I slipped below to check the chart.

Canal de las Ballenas was dead ahead. It would be a real challenge, a lot tougher than the canal we had just sailed through. Angel de la Guardia, an island close to the shore, formed the eastern side of the canal. It was forty miles long with steep sides and no possible anchorages that I could find on the chart. A major portion of the tide moved through this narrow canal which was over a thousand feet deep in some places. Its length was more than we could ever hope to sail during a single flood tide in a head wind. We could probably do it if the wind was behind us, but as usual, it was right on the nose. This would leave us sailing in the Ballenas Canal at night with an opposing tide, not in the best of circumstances, especially with no moon.

My thoughts were disrupted when the Bear was suddenly knocked down in a heavy gust. I looked out through the lee port lights into the water washing over them. A reef was tucked in, but that wasn't enough. We were being rapidly overwhelmed by the force of the wind. As the flood tide pushed hard against the north wind, a sea that had been just lumpy minutes ago quickly worked itself into steep swells with breaking crests.

Alarmed at how quickly the conditions were changing, I thought, "Don't break the boat! We've got to get out of this. It's way too much!"

Off to starboard a few miles away, Angel de la Guardia with its high rugged mountains stood as a sentinel. It might provide the shelter we desperately needed.

The Bear reached off downwind heading toward the island's southern tip as the wind continued to maul the boat. Bravely, the Bear struggled on dragging her boom in the water in the heavier gusts with the reefed main luffing to the battens.

As I looked anxiously ahead, the southern end of Angel la Guardia was a series of almost vertical cliffs dropping to a narrow sand beach below. It was a difficult struggle to sail the Bear in under the lee of the cliffs. She was viciously attacked by the full weight of the wind that pounced upon her from the high cliff tops above. After a serious struggle on the wet rolling deck, the anchor was lowered and holding with a six to one scope.

After the sails were furled and everything was put right, I sat in the cockpit for quite awhile as the gusts slammed the Bear with their persistent attacks.

Out beyond the protection of the cliffs, the Salsipuedes to leeward was totally wild, as the steep tumbling south bound seas collided with a strong north going flood.

We had only been sailing for an hour, but it felt like a hard day's sail and I was completely exhausted. It was nice just sitting in the cockpit as the angry little waves rushed along the hull. I looked forward to spending the rest of the day just resting and reading. This wind would surely blow itself out. I played with the idea of sailing around to the east side of the island just to see what it was like, but fatigue ruled that out.

Slipping below onto my bunk I began to read before drifting off with the book still in my hand. Hours later the roar of the wind broke through my deep sleep waking me with a start. Still half asleep, but already back in the cockpit, I reassured myself that nothing had changed. The Bear was right where she had been.

That afternoon I checked the chart and thought about sailing up the east side of Angel de la Guardia after the wind calmed. This would avoid the Ballenas Canal. At least the east side of the island offered available anchorages. However, we would have to wait until the weather improved. But if anything, the wind continued to increase.

It wasn't as if I hadn't seen this much wind before. I had sailed the schooner in similar winds, having been caught out in weather that became much worse than we ever expected. As the storm increased, the crew aboard the schooner had been sent below. Sitting in the cockpit, I sailed her under main and jib only. The wind driven spray, lifted from the water's surface, was thrown full force over the schooner at more than fifty miles an hour. It wasn't possible to look to windward in the gusts.

At one point the schooner was knocked flat. Instantly the lee rail disappeared, then the side deck, port lights, and hand rail on the cabin top went under as she gave way to the impact of the gust. The tiller was thrust to leeward into the water to the depth of my elbow before she began to fight her way back to the surface. With the mainsail eased and carrying a good luff we fought our way to safety. Later, after the schooner was berthed, we drove home. Passing a construction site, suddenly a tool shed began cart wheeling through a construction area and up over an eight foot cyclone fence landing in the street and narrowly missing our car.

"Well, that was some windy day," I replied in a light hearted manner, but to my surprise there was no comment from the crew, only deathly silence. No one aboard the schooner from that day on ever spoke of our adventure again.

I knew the Bear wasn't up to beating to weather in over fifty knots of wind, duck and cover was our reality now. Lie low and hold on.

My thoughts drifted back to the big anchor, and the day of its purchase as it continued to hold us safely. It was dark now as I peered out of the companionway into a black nothingness. The reality of dragging off into that blackness toward several unlit islands to our lee was more than I could ever possibly imagine.

The Bear, not being capable of carrying sail in these conditions, completely relied on her anchor. I was truly afraid now but the wind, indifferent to my fears, just continued to increase.

Attempting to distract myself, the RDF was tuned to a rock station in Dallas, but that didn't work. No source of entertainment could provide any assurance for what was happening now.

More furious than ever, the wind was determined to rip the Bear from its shelter under the towering cliffs and punish its skipper for so lightly messing about in the Sea of Cortez.

It was midnight now, and the wind had taken this struggle to a whole new level. It was unlike anything I've ever known. But still, the anchor held as I sat upright with a dry mouth and shaky hands on the bunk below. My float coat and harness were on and I was ready, but had no idea what to be ready for. As the gusts hit, the Bear reeled under their impact coming close to dipping her toe rail into angry waves now ripped from the water's surface and scattered to leeward as flying spray. Repeatedly, the stubborn anchor held its ground, consistently yanking the Bear's bow back to windward. "How hard is it blowing out there," I wondered? From experience I knew it was easily gusting at fifty or more under the shelter of the cliffs.

In a moment of bravado, I went to the companionway, headed topside to check the anchor rode for chafe as the wind continued to scream like a mad demon. When the next gust hit, the stainless steel tubing supporting the dodger I was standing under, flexed and twisted with the winds impact. I peeked cautiously around the dodger. There was nothing to be seen except for a few feet of deck and flying spray, illuminated through the ports by the gentle light of the kerosene lamps.

"Are you out of your mind! You could easily be blown off the boat in these gusts," I yelled at myself over the screaming wind. So it was go back, sit down, hang on, and pray all this would soon be over.

As I sat on the bunk, the air pressure in the cabin, driven by the heavy gusts, changed so rapidly that I began seeing double. I found this hard to believe and kept blinking to clear my vision.

By two in the morning, the wind began to slack off. An hour later I was asleep on the bunk, in full dress and ready for any event.

As I woke, the sun shone in brightly. Slowly, sitting up I listened for the wind, but there was none. As I peered out the port light, the Sea of Cortez looked just as it always had before the storm. It was as though that storm had been nothing more than a bad dream. But it was more than that. It was not a dream at all, but a test, and we had passed.

I had my life back and so did the Bear.

It was time to get out on the water. But really, all I wanted to do was lie around and rest, but that was no excuse. It was time to go. Truth be told, I really didn't want to haul the anchor up, figuring it must be too deeply set. I hauled in the chain until we were directly over the anchor and raised the mainsail. Then with both hands on the chain, I hauled giving it my best effort. At first it didn't move at all, but I kept the pressure on and after a few moments I felt it start to give. The anchor suddenly broke free, catching me by surprise as I stumbled backwards on the foredeck into the mast.

Moments later the anchor was on deck and in its chocks, but as I was tying it down I couldn't help notice the stock, the cross piece perpendicular to the flukes, was bent.

It took awhile to clear the south end of the island, just ghosting in the extremely light air. Once clear of the island, we started beating in equal tacks up the eastern shore of Angel de la Guarda. The wind continued to veer in our favor and we were soon able to sail one long tack up the shore. The breeze shifted favorably to a reach allowing the sails to be eased. The spinnaker was set at noon with the wind coming from behind.

After lunch, we continued run north along the shore for most of the afternoon in the light breeze. But by three o'clock the last of the wind dropped to zero leaving the spinnaker hanging like a curtain. Bringing the setting bag up onto the foredeck, I was able to carefully re-pack the spinnaker as it was slowly lowered into its setting bag. These conditions soon established a temporary routine when the the wind shut down at about the same time every afternoon for the next several days.

Once the spinnaker was stowed below, I would check the chart for an anchorage before getting the oar out. As I remember, the eastern shore of Angel la Guardia was quite beautiful with majestic scenery. Usually after an hour's workout with the oar we'd anchor in some quiet cove for the night.

Once the Bear was put to bed for the evening, I would leave the cockpit and settle in down below. From the job in the cockpit, to home in the cabin was no more than a few steps away. All this daily routine, was of course subject to whatever whims or mischief the Sea of Cortez could come up with. And past experience assured me that it would not disappoint!

20 SEVERAL NEAR DISASTERS

As we wandered north along the shore of Angel La Guardia, the days were quite routine on the surface. It was easy to get taken in by that, but the Sea of Cortez kept me on my toes, forcing me to keep my guard up. It was quite impossible to guess what would happen next as it was always hidden beneath the guise of routine. My only defense was to constantly stay on deck when the Bear was underway, or continue to rely on my intuition and be surprised by the unexpected.

Often I would read down below out of the intense sun and let the vane sail the boat. This worked well, but there were glitches in this plan. One morning the Bear sailed for an hour on the offshore tack before I tacked the boat then settled back down to read again. Somehow, the time got away from me.

I was lost in the story when an urgent thought broke through, "You'd better get up there," it demanded. Quickly moving to the cockpit I found the Bear innocently sailing into a shallow rocky cove. I stood transfixed for an instant, imagining the wreck that was about to take place before quickly releasing the vane and tacking back into deeper water. A new rule was imposed, never read down below on the inshore tack.

Several days later, I was down below again reading, this time on the offshore tack, when there was a scraping noise under the hull just before the Bear slowed, lifted her bow, and stopped dead in the water.

"What the Hell," I yelled to no one in particular. "We're in the middle of the Sea of Cortez, we can't be aground! It's a thousand feet deep here."

Pissed off, I rushed up the companionway scanning the full horizon. Nothing. Climbing out of the cockpit I walked forward to the bow thinking "What are you doing, there's nothing out here" until I leaned over and looked down under the bow at a large ball of kelp. Returning to the foredeck with the oar I went to work on the kelp until the Bear broke through and we were sailing again.

Several days later, I was reading down below again when the sound of breaking water got my attention. "Well, that's not right," I thought, "Better get up there." As I reached the cockpit more than a hundred or so Porpoises with grey backs and white underbellies passed close along both sides of the Bear on their way to somewhere. I watched them until they were gone, wondering where they were headed before returning to my reading.

The following day the wind was exceedingly light. I worked hard all day keeping the Bear moving, but our progress was so little that when we anchored for the night, I could still see our anchorage from the night before. A feeling of defeat swept over me, leaving me to think we'd never get to San Felipe. Moods do that.

The final day of our trek up the east side of Angel de la Guarda was a long one. The wind was very light, vanishing early in the afternoon and forcing me back to the oar. It was quite late before we finally arrived at Puerto Refugio.

Puerto Refugio is an interesting place and I had been looking forward to seeing it for some time. There was ample space for hundreds of yachts to anchor in the bay formed by three islands providing excellent shelter from almost any direction. I had been at the oar for hours and was exhausted. Not having the strength to explore other options, I picked the first anchorage we came to.

Our anchorage at Isla Granito was quite smelly and noisy. We were anchored only a hundred feet from a Sea Lion rookery. On the hill overlooking the sea lions was a pelican rookery.

As soon as the anchor went down the young Sea Lions came over to investigate. Darting about underwater, they charged the Bear's hull, abruptly turning away in a swish of bubbles only to pop up seconds later and look curiously at the boat as the big bulls continued to roar threateningly from the beach. Some porpoises flashed by, distracting the young sea lions, who chased after them doing a fine imitation of a porpoise leaping high above the surface to breathe.

Meanwhile, the pelicans in their rookery stood stoically on their hillside with their young all dressed in fluffy white down, blending perfectly among the stained rocks. The young quietly ambled about, looking for shade behind any cactus or rock not already occupied.

It was at Puerto Refugio that the Bear parted company with John Steinbeck's chosen route in the Log of the Sea of Cortez. His chartered boat, the Western Flyer, headed east from Refugio to mainland Mexico before eventually returning to Monterey, California.

During the night, the sea lion rookery finally quieted down somewhat which helped for sleeping, but as soon as I was seen on deck the following morning they all started in again.

There was a good breeze up, and it was a pleasure to get underway, if just for a fresh breath of sea air. The Bear began making good progress across the upper end of the Ballenas Canal. I was glad to have the wind. The breeze brought the temperature back down to manageable levels and the miles rolled off under the transom.

Life was good until halfway to the Baja shore when the wind stopped. It was a complete calm, just like someone had slammed the door on the wind. We sat mirrored on the water with limp hanging sails. There was not a sound in the complete silence except for my own movement about the boat.

As I looked across the vast empty sea, its light blue color contrasted nicely with the distant red mountains shimmering in the heat. The vast distances my eyes easily traveled only added to my sense of frustration at the loss of all progress. The points on the compass quietly swung past the lubber line, almost without notice, until the Bear pointed due south. Maybe she'd had quite enough of this Sea of Cortez business and just wanted to go home.

"Well, I give up," I thought. That was the best thing I could have done. Maybe, I could have rushed below for the oar, and used my frustration to confront this new difficulty, or I could just find something else to do. Checking the horizon, I searched for any sign of wind on the water but there was none. It was time to read. Later, I woke to find the book still in my hand and the sun low in the west. There was no chance of finding an anchorage for the night. Well, at least we were far enough from land not to be shoved ashore by the current.

I poured a glass of wine and turned on the direction finder for some music before starting dinner. Later, after the dishes were done, I returned to the cockpit. It had cooled off some but it was still glassy. The water's surface, still as a mirror, reflected the stars overhead. The Bear hung suspended in space with stars above and below. Sitting in the cockpit, I just took it all in, knowing that there would only be a slim chance I would ever experience this again.

The rattle of the main sheet blocks gently woke me. Just the slightest bit of breeze had the boat heading off to the southeast with its tiller locked. Being distracted at the time, I had forgotten to heave the boat to. After sorting the Bear out and checking my navigation, I returned to the cockpit to find the wind had completely disappeared again. Then, just as quickly it returned, but this time from the east, so the sails were trimmed and the Bear began to ghost northwest. Although we were sailing on course, I had no real idea where we were because the Bear had been sailing on her own for some time. However, I was pretty certain it would sort itself out in the daylight.

In the meantime, I stayed in the cockpit and sailed the boat as best I could. For the next ten hours I worked the Bear onward with an almost non-existent breeze coming from all points on the compass. Curious, I read the log and checked the mileage made good. Three miles, that was it. "Well, this is better than nothing, and after all, it all adds up," I rationalized, reluctantly concluding later that it would have been better to have slept the ten hours instead. As daylight arrived the wind began to fill in, and after several hours of fair sailing we'd covered more than twice the distance we had made in the previous ten hours.

We continued north along the Baja shore as the wind slowly veered into the west allowing me to slack the sails and reach. As I was having lunch, the usual red mountains I had taken for granted for months suddenly gave way to large rolling sand dunes, reminding me of the Arabian Desert.

This sudden change intensified my sense of self preservation, forcing me to check on my water. As I sounded the tank, it was almost empty. Two of the three remaining canisters were drained into the tank. Holding off on the final canister would be best, and the last two and a half gallons would serve as an emergency supply.

It was time to ration the water and pray for more wind. I thought about the rhyme of the Ancient Mariner I had read in high school. Just like in the poem, the wind remained very light, to nonexistent. The Bear sat hove to as we waited for further developments. After dinner, about eight-thirty, there was a slight rustle of sails and the boat swung to the whisper of new breeze that quickly died as I trimmed in the sails. Just a teaser I thought, before turning in for the night fully dressed and ready to sail at a moment's notice.

By eight-thirty the next morning we were underway again with a light easterly breeze that steadily developed into a ten knot southerly by mid afternoon. The spinnaker went up and we made good time in the steady wind. I took the spinnaker down just before dark.

Several hours later we arrived off Puertecitos which offered very limited protection from the southerly wind, but I decided to stop, rather than race on through the night.

I needed a break from that constant internal urge, continually pushing us ever onward. Jibing over in the dark, we sailed into Puertecitos. When the sounding line read twenty-five feet, the Bear spun up into the wind and the anchor was let go. Just to be safe, the anchor was set with a four to one scope and moments later was holding nicely in the sand bottom. The Sea of Cortez, being what it was, I didn't figure this wind would last and I was right. By midnight it had shifted into the west.

The wind continued to hum in the rigging throughout the night, and at times reached a high pitched screech. I slept soundly through it all, except to occasionally check on the Bear's position. The following morning, the wind had settled down to about ten knots. I completed the morning chores and did the laundry. The clothes that were hung in the rigging dried quickly in the desert wind. The rest of the day was spent catching up on reading and sleep. The bay at Puertecitos was lined with derelict house trailers sitting in the heat without any benefit of shade from the sun, resembling what I thought to be a desperate collection of retired Americans sheltering with limited means.

With the main luffing the following morning in the light breeze, I stood on the foredeck hauling up close to a hundred pounds of ground tackle. I couldn't help smiling as I thought back to San Diego, so long ago, when people would ask why on earth I needed such a big anchor.

This time the breeze was from the northeast at seven knots allowing us to reach up the coast. Once the Bear was on course and sailing, I went below to read. My latest book was 'Centennial' which I found very engaging. Deep into the book I suddenly looked up. "Check," flashed into my mind, "Check now!"

A moment later I was in the cockpit, and sure enough, we were sailing into trouble, headed for the beach with only several hundred feet to go. The wind had slowly changed direction taking the Bear along with it. It was funny, how early in the cruise I had developed a sub-conscience sense of danger. By now, it seemed almost instinctive. I likened it to being a wolf in a den, where every little sound would instinctively open one of its yellow eyes.

Later, after the cruise, I read books from other single handed sailors who had also experienced this ability and had written about it. The wind held well into the night before it gave out completely. The Bear was hove to, just at the onset of the ebb. As it got light the following morning I was busy at work figuring out how much damage had been done to our progress north, due to the south bound ebb and came to the conclusion we had lost six miles in the calm.

It took all the following morning to earn that distance back in the light contrary air. As we continued along Baja's eastern coast, I noticed what appeared to be more wind closer in to shore. Without thinking I tacked in toward it, then suddenly ran aground in muddy water more than a mile from the beach. Fortunately the tide was flooding, but it still took a lot of work to get off.

The Bear was heeled over by the force of the flooding tide. I looked down at the rudder as the water poured around it and estimated the speed of the current at about two knots. After the sails were lowered, the Avon inflatable was pulled from its box and pumped up. A kedge with its ground tackle was brought up from down below and cleated to the Bear before being put into the Avon. I rowed the anchor out and set it before returning to the boat. After tying off the Avon, I began hauling the Bear off the mud backwards into deeper water. It didn't take long before she was afloat. Soon the anchor was up and we were sailing again with the Avon in tow. This grounding was a wakeup call. Even though we were still in the Sea of Cortez, we were really sailing in the Colorado River Delta. The wind steadied a bit and veered into the south, allowing me to set the spinnaker as we ran north toward San Felipe.

As I remember, the sky was overcast in thin clouds allowing the sun to shine through the old baby blue spinnaker that had made our progress so much easier. I sat in the cockpit sailing for the rest of the afternoon with the sounding line next to me, filled with conflicting thoughts about the cruise.

I didn't want this cruise to end. It was like the feeling I would get in college when taking a final exam and the professor said, "Time's up." I wanted a do over, even though I knew it wasn't possible. I wanted a second chance. This was supposed to be the hallmark cruise but it wasn't, and I couldn't let that go. There were too many errors.

This cruise would be over today. That was a fact. The San Felipe lighthouse had already appeared off in the distance. Reluctantly, I went forward and released the guy before stowing the pole on the mast. The spinnaker came down and was neatly packed into its setting bag for the last time. The jib was lowered and furled on the foredeck before making the anchor ready just as we entered the harbor.

With the anchor and main down, we were safe within the harbor after two-thousand two-hundred miles of real adventure. As the Bear sat quietly at anchor, I sat almost motionless in the cockpit mulling over all that had happened during the cruise. There was no applause, no cheering, I was alone, sitting with quiet thoughts. We were actually in San Felipe! It was over.

The fulfillment of this cruise, even as it stood, was a great accomplishment. It was far beyond what I had ever done before, far beyond all the college degrees and sailing races I've ever won. Never had I experienced so much resistance and struggled so hard to successfully complete this cruise. Intuitively, I knew this cruise would become a foundation for even greater achievements to come.

21 HOMEWARD BOUND

The harbor at San Felipe had a rather unused look about it. Consisting of nothing more than a rock seawall, it enclosed a stretch of open beach serving only as shelter or a hiding place from storms. There were no facilities within the harbor and few people to be seen. Three fishing boats, in a somewhat dejected state, were moored stern first to the rock wall with bow anchors out. Of those three, one had sunk leaving only its wheel house and spars above the surface.

Over on the beach, an abandoned yacht, about thirty feet long, sat high above the tide line lying on her side. The sun had done its damage, to the point where one could easily see through the hull seams. My best guess was that its owner had just walked away.

When I called hauling companies in San Diego, before sailing into Mexico, I was told they refused to do business south of the border and referred me to a small independent trucker. Back in February when Paul became my hauler, Paul said he'd modify his trailer for sailboats. Paul was the only offer I had. Somewhere along the way Paul's phone number had been lost and now I was completely dependent upon him to show up, and that worried me.

The town of San Felipe was more than a mile up the beach from the harbor. I was ready for some civilization. Anything that took my mind off worrying about Paul not showing up would be a welcome diversion.

The following morning I pulled the Avon far up on the rocks and rolled it over to cover the oars before tying its painter around a boulder to secure it.

As I headed along the beach, the tide was out, leaving more than a hundred yards of hard packed sand between the dunes and sea. The low tide made for easy walking.

After going some distance along the beach, It occurred to me that I had to keep a hand in my pocket to hold my pants up. Apparently, I had lost a lot of weight. Being so preoccupied with sailing, I had never given much thought to my weight. Much later, after finding a scale, I found I had lost twenty pounds. So much for the healthy benefits of my cooking! Something had to be done, so in the remaining days before Paul's planned arrival I had breakfast out. The steak and eggs seemed to help.

Continuing my walk along the beach, I came to an RV campground about the size of a football field filled with people from the States. Most of the people had dune buggies and used them for transportation around town or for recreation on the nearby dunes.

San Felipe was a good sized town with paved streets. There were many shops and restaurants including a "Washamatica" for doing clothes. It was clear that American tourism was responsible for much of the town's prosperity. In the days that followed I was able to explore the area in a more thorough fashion.

One of the most interesting excursions led me out to the lighthouse located on a small peninsula called Punta San Felipe. The lighthouse was very prominent, painted white with a black top. As I came nearer, there was a sheltered lagoon in its lee filled with half-sunk or beached fishing boats that had out lived their usefulness. Off to one side, there was a boat yard with two boats under construction.

Not far from the lighthouse was a humble fisherman's shrine with white walls and a terra cotta roof. Inside its gated alcove stood the statue of a Saint. From what I could make out from the placard, it was a shrine for fisherman. Others had thrown money through the gate to the Saint. I was very touched by this and felt compelled to do the same. "Thanks," I said humbly, " For letting me off the hook for all those mistakes out on the water."

As I headed back down the hill from the lighthouse there was a wharf on the windward side of the peninsula that I hadn't noticed before. It served the fishing industry in the northern gulf providing fuel, water, and ice.

Continuing back to the boat, I wandered through the RV camp that I had passed earlier and discovered a pay shower. This was an excellent find, and I couldn't have been more pleased than if I had discovered King Tut's Tomb. The last real shower I had was in San Diego more than four months ago. For the rest of the day I looked forward to a shower, knowing I'd return again the following day.

All this time, I had been showering out of a bucket using seawater, a washcloth, and lemon scented dish detergent. It is remarkable what dish detergent can do to hair. Mine was now bleached the color of straw and was just about as difficult to manage.

As the days went by, I became more and more anxious as I waited for the truck driver. Then one morning, quite suddenly, there was a yell from ashore. "Hello the boat. Are you the guy waiting for the truck?" After waving a hand, I boarded the Avon and in a short while we were talking on the seawall. Paul laid out the plan. He had arrived the day before and made arrangements for the haul out. I asked him where we would haul the Bear and he said on the beach near the lighthouse.

The trailer would be run down the beach at low tide. Once the Bear was on the trailer it would be pulled up the beach over old aircraft gratings with a winch on a 1942 Dodge Power Wagon. Then we'd lower the mast, tie everything down and be on our way. It sounded simple.

Before Paul left to confirm his arrangements he said, "If anybody asks, tell them that I'm just a friend helping out. The Mexicans don't allow American companies to come down here and do business anytime they want. It's all very complicated." I spent the rest of the day worried about how many things could go wrong.

After clearing the harbor the following morning, we ghosted north along the coast in light winds until I saw the trailer on the beach out in the water. Paul had been waiting for me. The Dodge truck was also there, high up on the beach, with its long cable connected to the trailer. I sailed in as close to the trailer as possible before anchoring. It would be at least an hour before the tide would be high enough to cover the trailer so we went off to breakfast.

When we returned, the water was up to the top of the trailer's support pads used to hold the boat upright. I rowed out to the Bear and got the mainsail up. Paul motioned me in. The Bear glided right up onto the trailer

I quickly climbed down into the water and onto the trailer. We each took a side and began screwing the jacks up to bring the support pads against the hull. The Bear began to bump and bang against the pads in the sloppy water, but we continued until the Bear was solidly secured.

Slowly the old Dodge Power Wagon began to winch the boat up the beach. Occasionally we'd have to move the aircraft gratings in front of the trailer's wheels to keep them from bogging down in the wet sand. After an hour of steady progress the Bear was safely in the parking lot and hitched behind the tow vehicle.

It was mid-morning and rapidly warming up as we began to dismantle the boat for travel. The mast proved to be a problem. We moved the boat over to a building with a second story balcony. A volunteer from the crowd of spectators helped control the upper part of the mast from the balcony as we lowered it down. After five hours of continuous work in the overwhelming heat, the Bear was finally ready to hit the road to San Diego.

Not so fast, I thought. It's not all downhill from San Diego. There's Point Conception to sail around and six hundred miles of hard sailing to windward before we're back on the bay. I know what the Bear can do, but is she even up to that kind of sailing? Am I? My imagination began to run wild with thoughts of long periods without sleep, sailing through fog, waves, and high winds as large container ships lurked about. But before dealing with that, first we had to get back to San Diego.

The truck pulled the Bear through San Felipe onto north bound highway five. The wind blowing in through the truck's open windows felt good after such a long hot struggle with the boat. Finally, the Bear was on her way home.

All that worry about the trucker not coming, or being unable to haul the Bear safely was thankfully put behind, just like so much road passing in the truck's rear view mirror. There wasn't much traffic as we crossed the sparse desert driving through the monotony and heat along the featureless well worn two lane road. The distant mountains ahead slowly shifted into what I thought to be my own country. Stopping for gas temporarily broke the monotony, but we were soon back at it again. After all those months in Mexico it felt good to be coming home. Several hours later we lined up with the other north bound traffic for crossing the border at Mexicali.

The Mexican border guard asked the same routine questions that I had often heard throughout the cruise before waving us on toward the U.S. crossing at Calexico.

I've always felt, for some reason, that it's more difficult to get back into my own country than into others when traveling. This probably has something to do with drugs and the profiling of people who are likely to use them. We went through the usual round of questions as the border guard viewed us suspiciously. There was a tense moment when the guard casually sniffed along the edge of the driver's window, making me wonder just how far he would go with his search. He walked back and took a look at the Bear before waving us on. Surprisingly, he didn't even climb up and look into the Bear. It probably was too much effort, but whatever the reason, I was relieved when he told us to drive on. Suddenly, after crossing the border, I felt everything would be much easier now that we were back in the States.

Later over dinner at a Denny's restaurant, I asked Paul how much pot he thought the Bear could hold. He didn't have an answer, but I wondered if smuggling could possibly be this easy. However, I wasn't tempted to try it. My personal freedom was worth too much, far more than any profit that could be made from smuggling.

We took our time over dinner. Paul wanted to leave late so we could get over the Tecate Mountains in darkness to avoid overheating the truck's engine. Paul was very careful about planning and managing his equipment. As it worked out, we arrived in San Diego just before midnight after a long slow haul up over the mountains. It had been a very full day. Paul slept in his truck and I had my usual bunk in the Bear, after shifting the wind vane and other gear for the needed space.

The following day was Sunday so we were held over until Monday when the local boat yard would lift the Bear off the trailer and re-launch her. At least that was the plan, until I spent Sunday contemplating other possibilities during a long walk.

Did I want to spend a month beating my way back up the California coast through wind, fog, and shipping, or would I rather spend my time back on San Francisco Bay for the summer? After thinking about those steep cresting waves off Point Conception and the thirty knot winds that went with them, compared with those quiet restful delta nights, filled with the sounds of bull frogs and crickets, quickly provided a practical answer.

Reminiscing back to when we passed Point Arguello headed south, I reminded myself about what I had said out loud, "There's no way a Bear can beat back through that," as I watched the next big sea pass under us. And that cinched it. A phone call would be made, and there would be a change of plans if I could get the money.

Later that afternoon I talked it over with Paul and he agreed to haul the boat to Alameda for four hundred dollars. For me, it was cheap at that price, considering what I'd be getting. So Monday became a driving day, punctuated only by stops for fuel and food as we slowly worked our way around the Los Angeles Basin before stopping after dark at a rest stop near King City.

Tuesday went pretty much the same, with a long drive up the Salinas Valley with its pleasant scenery before arriving in Watsonville early that afternoon. Arrangements had been made for me to pick up the money I needed to pay Paul for his services. Heading north again, we slowly worked our way through the Santa Cruz Mountains, then over a maze of urban freeways, before finally arriving in Alameda at Svend's Boat Works. The following morning the Bear was lifted off the trailer and Paul headed back to San Diego.

Financial problems began to loom large. My last paycheck would come at the end of July. That check, for half pay, would have to be stretched until the end of September. Foreseeing this problem early helped, but it would still take some serious financial maneuvering. At least there was enough food left in the Bear to last through September.

In the meantime, I did a quick haul out at Svend's Boat Yard. The Bear got a fresh coat of paint on her topsides and some bottom paint when I wasn't busy varnishing. All painting and varnishing had to be done selectively, usually early in the morning to avoid the pollution whose main source came from the sandblasting of boat bottoms. Gone were the Bear's sun and salt bleached white decks, now turned to a shabby grey. The grime had even begun to penetrate down below making living aboard difficult in spite of the boat being closed up. This was a busy time, and time is money, so I pushed hard to get the mast up and the boat back in the water.

The day before the scheduled launch I grabbed my laundry bag late in the afternoon and headed for a laundromat on Park Street. Once the laundry was done, I bought a snack for dinner from the local fast food place before heading back to the boat.

It was dark when I returned to the boat yard. Suddenly taken aback, I stood there under the street lamp and peered in through the locked gate that blocked the entrance. There was no one in the guard shack, or even anyone in sight. My choice was to wait until daylight or climb over the gate. After waiting for awhile with still no one around, the laundry bag was tossed over the fence before I followed it. As I started toward the Bear, the security guard who had been in the shadows all along began following me in his truck while I walked in the glare of his headlights.

After reaching the boat, I stopped and walked back to the truck.

"Why are you following me," I asked.

"I'm the security guard here."

"Why didn't you just open the gate?"

"I'm not supposed to do that. I don't let people in. As far as I'm concerned you're a trespasser and if you don't leave I'll call the police."

"Look, that's my boat," I said, pointing at the Bear. "It's where I live."

"If you don't leave, I'll call the police."

"Well, I'm not leaving. Go ahead and call. At least you'll know where I am when they arrive. Right now I'm turning in."

And with that, I climbed up the ladder into the Bear's cockpit, opened the hatch and dropped down below, before sliding it closed behind me. Sunlight permeated the cabin the following morning as I opened my eyes. Images flashed through my mind about last night. Well, I thought, at least I'm not in jail.

It was a busy morning and I was in a rush to finish last minute details. Just before lunch, the yard crew picked up the Bear with the transporter so I could finish painting the bottom where the supports had been. The paint was dry by the time lunch was over, and the boat was launched. She was sculled over to a convenient berth. As the ebb was already running it would be best to quickly get underway. Down below, the floor boards had been pulled up making it easy to check the bilge for leaking, but there was very little water. After the boat was washed down and the yard bill was paid, we cast off.

The Bear was finally back in home waters again. An hour later found us beating down the last of the Oakland Estuary dodging tugs and a container ship that was docking. Once back in open water I made myself a snack as we passed under the Bay Bridge. We took Yerba Buena and Treasure Island to port, sailing in their lee, then rounded up at the north east corner of Treasure Island, sailing hard on the wind into the normal San Francisco Bay summer conditions.

In no time, spray was rattling down on the cabin top and streaming off the lower part of the mainsail. That water was cold, way different than in Mexico. Quickly, I put the tiller lock on adjusting it for weather helm and slacked the main to balance the boat, before retreating to the comfort of the cabin. The Bear headed toward Angel Island with its lee rail just skimming the bay's choppy surface.

I kept an eye on our progress as I made coffee sitting under the protection of the dodger. There was no telling what might pop out of that dense fog streaming in under the Gate. It was thick enough to hide the city's waterfront with the exception of the skyscrapers that towered above it. As the Bear sailed on, she headed up in the gusts and fell off in the lulls as the ebb continually pushed her to windward allowing us to pass between Alcatraz and Angel island, then to windward of Raccoon Straits, before slipping into sunny Richardson's Bay on one tack.

Being acclimated to the Sea of Cortez, I didn't return to the cockpit until the wind and waves had calmed down. It was a pleasure to sit in the cockpit in the warmth of the afternoon sun as the Bear made her final approach to her home port of Sausalito. Filled with emotion, I watched my old haunts slowly come into focus. A group of Folkboats and Knarrs were sailing along the Sausalito shore, headed for the Wednesday night races off the foggy San Francisco waterfront.

The sun, well to the west, shaded Sausalito's fog capped hills as it always does in the late afternoon. It made for a nice welcome and the best homecoming I could have had. The wind, much lighter now, shaped our course into the shallow waters just east of the Sausalito channel to avoid the ebb pushing out of Richardson's Bay. Slowly, we worked our way deeper into the bay against the tide before finally short- tacking up the narrow channel leading into the shallow basin that harbored the Sausalito Cruising Club sitting on its old wooden barge.

I had finally returned. The Bear was secured exactly where she had been on the day we first began this cruise eight months earlier. It was an emotional moment for me as I sat quietly in the Bear's cockpit. The sailing had been difficult, to say the least, but all the challenges had been met.

Everything I needed for finishing the sabbatical project had been achieved, and during the coming school year my project would be used in sixth grade classes for Social Studies.

I glanced up at the Bear's starboard spreader where a somewhat battered Cruising Club burgee had flown steadily through thousands of miles of sailing. It was my way of saying thanks to the Sausalito Cruising Club for allowing me to use their float as I prepared for the cruise. Finally, with a feeling of accomplishment and a strong sense of pride, I stepped off the boat and went for a walk along Bridgeway, Sausalito's main street. Tourists and locals crowded the sidewalks and stores as usual. Sausalito was the same as always, nothing had changed except me. Inwardly, I felt strong and full of confidence.

As I walked on, my thoughts turned to an Irish coffee and a good view of the city at sunset. However, that was not to be. As I strolled past the No Name Bar, Bill Jelliffe rushed out and caught my arm. This wasn't the best timing for me. I always needed extra time to bolster myself up and prepare for Bill. Bill is a larger than life character, actively engaged in any pursuit that grabs his attention, whereas I tend to hold back and prefer to observe life. It always helps when I'm prepared beforehand so as not to be overwhelmed by his enthusiasm.

Bill and I are constant competitors on both land and sea. This is not an exaggeration. If not competing while racing on the bay, then some form of competition will occur at the yacht club bar or anywhere else we happen to be. Our competition mostly concerns things nautical. It's not that we're antagonistic. Actually, we have great respect for each other, even while arguing hard to make a winning point.

Bill is also a Bear skipper. He sails Puff, Bear number fifty-nine, if memory serves correctly. Bill is also involved with saving old neglected Bears, collecting them as if they were stray cats, then redistributing them to a fresh clientele, who thanks to Bill's persuasion, eagerly become their new custodians.

Years ago, long after I had sold my Bear, Bill rushed up to me from out of nowhere and said, "Hey Dave, you want to buy a Bear for a dollar?" "Bill," I said, "You mean ten thousand dollars. You know I'll put at least that much into it." Bill just laughed.

Outside the bar, Bill persuaded me to come into the No Name. "Come on in and I'll buy you a drink." You can tell us how the cruise went. We were just talking about you!"

"I'm pretty tired right now Bill, can't we do this another time?"

"Aw, you can sleep anytime, this is more important, people want to meet you. Right now you're the talk of the town!"

I doubted that. "Well, ok," I said, as I felt the last of my resistance crumble.

When I first saw Bill I knew I had been caught. We went back into the No Name, and Bill bought me an Irish coffee. We sat down at his table where he was holding court with a mixed group of characters whom I had often seen in the past prowling about the docks. Silently, they sat nursing their beers sizing me up before Bill spoke again.

"So, how was the cruise?"

"It was good," I said, and went on to tell them about all the places I stopped and the storms along the way, avoiding the near disasters such as almost wrecking the boat or falling overboard, and other such screw ups, etcetera, etcetera. When I had finished my story there were the usual questions about navigation, provisions, why no motor, and the Mexican authorities.

Finally the conversation drifted off to other sailing things. "Hey," Bill said, "Do you still carry your spinnaker pole up on the mast? You know that's no good for racing. It disturbs the wind flow over the mainsail." Yeah, the others chimed in while looking over to see what I'd say to that. "Well, that's true," I said, "But the system is faster and easier to use, so I'll stick with it." Some of the others were immediately skeptical, but Bill completely disagreed and wanted to argue the subject further, but I said, "You do it your way Bill, but I'll see you out on the race course." That got a loud jeer from the bunch at the table, who'd had who knows how many beers before I had arrived, giving me the opening I needed to make my escape. Out on the street, the cool night air felt good as I headed back to the boat. I was tired. It had been a long day. But as I walked along Bridgeway I thought more about Bill. He always kept his ear to the wharf, so to speak, and knew exactly what went on in the wooden boat community. Not long after I bought the Bear, Bill came to ask a favor of me. He had found out that the schooner I had sold earlier didn't have a skipper for the upcoming Master Mariners Regatta. Fortunately for Bill, the new owner sadly didn't know how to sail. Bill wanted my recommendation to skipper the schooner before the new owner would give him the ok. I gave him my approval and we shook hands on it. Overtime, Bill became the schooner's full time skipper.

Bill in the white hat.

Shaking hands with Bill is no small thing. It's a serious matter. From my point of view strength and speed are mandatory, just like at the start of a high school wrestling match. There's the stance, with feet well planted for balance, the leaning in, showing intent, the minor tensing of the fingers instantly before finding your adversaries weakness, then plunging in, grasping your opponent's hand in a death grip just before he tries to do the same to yours. Of course the object of this contest was to avoid becoming a victim of Bill's vise-like hand.

Oh yes, and then there are the facial expressions which seal the deal, meaning that come hell or high water, no matter what, the agreement must be carried out. During the hand shake Bill's face is filled with determination and commitment, whereas mine is usually a grimace, because once again, I just wasn't fast enough at the grip.

Throughout the time I was lucky enough to know him, Bill never faltered on a hand shake over money or for any other reason. As energetic as Bill was, without meaning to, he could take a lot out of you, especially if you lived the quiet life of a gentle observer.

Back at the club, the Bear piped her skipper aboard with a slight curtsey as he stepped on deck, before quietly slipping below in full retreat.

.

22 BACK IN HOME WATERS

A Delta cruise is a longtime tradition with me. Having the summers off, thanks to teaching, allows for precious time needed to maintain my boat and cruise in the Delta. Having those summers off isn't a paid vacation. Teachers are paid only for the days they work. Being in the Delta will help cut expenses and allow me to spend time with friends who also cruise there during their vacations.

The San Joaquin and Sacramento Rivers flow west down from the Sierra Nevada Mountains. Their journey takes them across the Sacramento Valley to form the Delta which consists of many small sloughs and islands, then moves on through Suisun, San Pablo, and San Francisco Bays, before emptying into the sea.

It took several days to make the Bear ready for the cruise. Small details were attended to and my onboard supplies were supplemented with special items I enjoy. Finally, everything was good to go except for my skiff which looked very shabby. While I had been in Mexico, it had been run down by a fishing boat. Fortunately, a friend had rescued it. The damage wasn't too serious, but it would require attention once I returned from the Delta.

We set out in somewhat ideal conditions, except for the fact that there wasn't much wind in Richardson Bay. It was still early and the normal wind pattern hadn't filled in yet. Waiting for the wind was not an option. The flood tide was just beginning to run and we couldn't afford to miss it. The oar was brought out and put to good use.

It wasn't the first cruise to the Delta that had started this way. During the twelve or so years I had sailed into the Delta only half of those cruises were done with an engine.

At this point the water was slack in Richardson Bay. We made good time under oar, finding catspaws here and there to sail in before discovering a back eddy at Tiburon Point that shoved us out into Raccoon Strait where the flood tide took over.

The winds remained light as we crossed the shipping channel headed toward Richmond. Ships are always a concern, but fortunately this time there were none to be seen. With fog on the coast, I thought, it was just a matter of time before the wind would increase. However, my expectation of more wind only led to disappointment. Sailing around the Brothers, a group of rocky islands, took some planning. Given the fast currents and light winds, it took some work with the oar to avoid being swept into them. Of course, towing the skiff didn't make sailing in these conditions any easier.

Now that we were in San Pablo Bay, there was plenty of space to fly the spinnaker and let the wind vane do the sailing. Once the spinnaker was up and drawing, I settled back and made some coffee. It felt good to stand in the cockpit with a cup of coffee in one hand and wave to a passing sloop headed back down to the bay under power. We continued to carry the spinnaker across San Pablo Bay all the way into Carquinez Strait. With several jibes coming up, the spinnaker was dropped to avoid the extra foredeck work as we navigated our way through the straits. By mid-afternoon the light air had began to fade about the time we arrived off the Martinez Marina.

It didn't make sense to continue on into Suisun Bay. We were in no hurry so we headed into the marina and were assigned a berth for the night. Our berth was a side tie downwind. Getting into it was a bit challenging, making me drop all sail some distance from the berth in a dead end fairway. There was little room for mistakes, but we made a good landing. Sitting in the cockpit with a glass of wine, I entertained myself planning how I might get out of this miserable berth the following day. With the wind as it was, it was impossible to sail out.

Several solutions came to mind: Casting out an anchor and kedging off, towing the Bear out with the skiff, or sculling the Bear out, but none of the above choices sounded like anything I wanted to do. What I was really looking for was a little magic just to make everything easier. "Well, dream on," I thought. Little did I know it at the time, but the following day would provide unthought-of of possibilities.

Before the evening was over the Bear gave considerably better than she got in a scuffle with a hapless motorboat that blundered into her stainless steel bow roller. The motorboat limped off in full retreat without any apology given.

The next morning we were on the mud. Taking a depth sounding in the berth last night would have been a good idea, but I forgot. Perhaps settling in with a glass of wine after tying up was a bit premature given the circumstance. How embarrassing! You would think when you rented a slip for the night that the water would be deep enough, but just the same, it was still the skipper's fault. Now there was nothing to do but sit around and wait as passers-by asked dumb questions, such as why the Bear's ass is up higher than her bow. Sulking silently, the Bear had no sympathy for me whatsoever and let me know it. She made it clear that she had seen better skippers.

My personal strategy was to pretend the grounding didn't happen. I got busy and made some coffee and offered a cup to a nice looking lady on a Pacific Sea Craft twenty-five, called Yankee Dew, which had the good fortune to be afloat like all the other boats in the marina. I was invited aboard. We exchanged names and began a pleasant conversation. Sure enough, it was not long before someone came down the dock and asked where the skipper of the grounded boat was. "I think he's up at the showers," I said, implying I was not the Bear's skipper. Lin gave me a "Hey wait a minute look," but quickly forgave my transgression seeing the humor in the situation. Later the Bear floated off unnoticed as Lin and I were still deep in conversation.

A friendship had blossomed as we commiserated with each other over our current problems. As the day moved on, it became quite warm. I noticed there wasn't any wind and commented to Lin that I wouldn't be going anywhere soon.

Lin, who was headed home to Pittsburg, offered me a tow which was gladly accepted. Now, because of the calm, I found it easy to scull the Bear out of the marina. We connected a towline and headed out.

From here on, a lot of maneuvering would be needed in the narrow shipping channel to avoid the shoals in Suisun Bay. This bay was tricky to sail in. It had a depth of less than ten feet at low water leaving large areas that dried out in its center called Middle Ground. Most yachtsmen don't like Suisun Bay and usually motor through it staying strictly in the deep water channel for shipping. Off in the distance, the twin towers of the power plant at Pittsburg shimmered in the heat as we steadily motored toward them. It was late afternoon before we were finally able to put the towers behind us and arrive at the Pittsburg Marina. The towline was cast off just before the entrance making it easy for me to scull slowly up to the guest dock.

Lin came over after securing Yankee Dew. We exchanged a few words of parting before she left to return to her world. Lin's cruise was over and the real world with its challenges beckoned. She would go home and assume her responsibilities as a mother and wife. My real world beckoned too, but I could still hold it at bay for awhile longer.

Later I walked into town to have dinner at the New Mecca, a Mexican restaurant Lin had recommended. The food was quite good. By mid- morning the following day, a light wind was blowing out of the east. Even with the wind against us, it was a relief to get out of the stifling marina. The cloudy sky and light breeze, unusual for this time of the year, made for a sultry heat that continued to thwart the cooler northwesterly breeze I had counted on.

Our destination was Seven Mile Slough. It's amazing what the flood tide can do for you when you sail with it. As you sail toward the Delta, the tide can last for ten hours or more if you have good wind, but as you head back down to the bay, the best you can hope to get from an ebb tide is about four and a half hours.

Planning a destination and actually getting there are two different things, so I had no real idea where we might end up for the night, but knew we'd have to get off the San Joaquin River to find a safe anchorage. Seven Mile Slough seemed logical.

I think this is what bothers most sailors with engines, they must get from A to B, on their imposed time schedule, but that's just my opinion. Sailing is really easier when you apply an engine as needed, almost everybody knows that, except for a few of us. Sometimes, when down below in the evenings, I would think about living life on the water and being as free as the wind. It was a comforting feeling being independent of modern technology, but as you have seen from my past experience, it can be a hard life and a risky one, though it has its rewards.

As the sun lowered in the west, it took the last of the wind with it making for the beginning of a beautiful sunset. The Bear drifted sideways to her intended course in the quiet water that mirrored her sails and pink clouds above. Small pieces of driftwood and weed lay scattered about on the water released from the shore by the flood tide in a golden calm of twilight. Slack water had set in. Our Seven Mile Slough destination was reachable with a little work and would provide a safe haven.

After locking the tiller in place, a tow line was rigged to the skiff and I began pulling the Bear. This can be rewarding and is something sailors unknowingly miss when using an engine. From where I sat in the skiff, the Bear looked beautiful under tow, gracefully gliding along under full sail in the sunset. There isn't anything quite as nice as watching your boat on the water. After a bit of effort at the oars, we were off the narrow entrance to the slough. Bringing the skiff alongside, I collected the tow line and climbed aboard. The jib was lowered and furled. The oar was brought out and the Bear was once again underway. The skiff slipped aft, obediently taking her place behind the Bear as we entered the slough, sculling toward the small marina some distance off.

Passing a farm house half hidden behind the levee, a screen door slapped closed in the twilight and the voice of a small child called out, "Look! A man is rowing a boat."

About halfway to the dock I stopped. The mainsail was lowered and furled before I took up the oar again to scull the remaining distance. Once settled in, the awning was put up to keep the evening dew off and a glass of wine was poured.

From the cockpit the view was delightful as the very last of the twilight silhouetted the large oak trees on the slough's levee. Looking down below, the amber glow from the kerosene lamps reflected off the cabin sides. All was at peace except for the bull frogs and crickets warming up for the oncoming night.

The first of the evening breeze stirred faintly. Little catspaws came and went on the slough's glassy surface leaving small wavelets to occasionally collide with the Bear's hull in a soft lapping sound. After all those miles of tough sailing during the Mexican cruise we had found peace. I had been looking forward to this moment for such a long time. When times were difficult during the cruise I often thought of the Delta in twilight.

As I sat thinking quietly in the Bear's cockpit, I knew it was time to put to rest the problems that had driven me to make this cruise. Even now, solutions came as vague feelings. Putting those solutions into words gave them definition and power, but once acted upon, gave them the finality of consequences. Was I ready to take that on? I was running out of time. Action needed to be taken. There was one other thing, but I couldn't quite put my finger on it, and at this point it was holding me back. I still wasn't comfortable with the way I had sailed during the cruise, but didn't know why.

The next morning found the Bear reaching out of Seven Mile Slough onto the San Joaquin River. It was a beautiful day, full of possibilities. No decision had been made yet about where we were going as we ran with the breeze upriver. It was as though a leaf had fallen from a tree into the water to be blown about by a capricious breeze. But in time, I sensed that mindless leaf was headed toward Potato Slough, and coincidentally, so was the Bear.

As we headed into Potato at midday, the jib was doused, and the anchor made ready. The anchorage was crowded as I rounded the point and only one spot was open. It was known as the hole, a place where anchors dragged. Most skippers familiar with the anchorage avoided it when they could.

Along the shore to windward were a row of boats that faced bow in with stern anchors out. Various dinghies and water toys were scattered between the moored boats. On board the larger boats, people were sheltering from the heat with iced drinks under awnings. Such luxuries were nice when they worked. When they didn't, they became the foundation of endless conversation. Everyone had an opinion on how to manage a fix.

But now that we've been seen, the topics would drift and the kibitzing would begin. Kibitzing is a natural sport among those already anchored. I've often enjoyed it myself, but we weren't anchored now and the focus was on us. It's a karmic thing, you get back what you give out. How well a skipper handles his boat can be the measure of his credibility within the group. It was quite unusual for boats to enter this crowed anchorage under sail. This would double the attention we were getting. Many of those arm chair skippers who had secretly dreamed of anchoring under sail were now taking notice.

However, if you manage to snag someone's anchor line, then drag their boat along with yours head long into the tules, you'd better run for it as soon as you can. Your opinion won't be worth much. Apologizing will gain very little. Snobbery among sailors is usually about ownership, however, there is a portion of it that's about sailing skill too. Don't ask me how I learned that. "Damn kid, should'a used his engine!"

Knowing we were under the gun, we did our best. Sailing to lee of the other anchored boats and in close to the tules, the Bear gained momentum before coming head to wind. Then she glided to a stop over the hole just before the anchor was lowered. As we fell back in the light breeze, the Bear's bow was firmly pulled up to windward with less than a three to one scope. It was the big anchor that made us look good. Within a few minutes, there was a neat harbor furl in the mainsail and the awning was up. Not seeing any familiar boats, I poured a glass of wine and settled into the cockpit with a good book for the rest of the day.

It's my habit to go for an early morning row before the water is shredded by powerboats. It's the best time of the day when everything is still cool and quiet. I would stick close to the fringes of the slough watching for the occasional muskrat or beaver leaving its gentle vee shaped wake, or wayward fenders that have drifted away from other boats in the anchorage. Occasionally, I would find something of value that needed to be returned.

I was on the Sacramento River years ago during an early morning row. After passing under the bridge at Steamboat Slough I turned the skiff into the current and headed close inshore past a small motorboat anchored with its occupants still asleep. Portions of the levee alongshore were thickly wooded and I enjoyed exploring them. After awhile, I grew tired and let the skiff drift back on the current past the small motorboat. A young woman was in its cockpit fishing topless. "Good morning," I said. Startled, she reached for something to cover up, but shrugged and thought better of it. She returned my greeting, smiled, and got on with her fishing.

After awhile, a daily routine emerges when at anchor. Most chores are done after breakfast before it gets hot. The lamps and stove are topped up with fuel. Water is transferred to the tank from the canisters when necessary, brass is polished as needed, along with other housekeeping choirs. After a light lunch, the boat is washed down not only to keep it cool from the relentless sun, but also to keep its seams tight. That was a lesson I had learned the hard way.

It was my first year cruising as a skipper in the Delta. Sue, my wife, and I had spent a month up on Steamboat Slough. Our Folkboat was seldom washed down and its hull seams had opened up. It was something I wasn't aware of until we sailed home. Occasionally, sailing home goes easily, but this wasn't one of those times. As we beat down Suisun Bay in thirty knots of wind, those dried out hull strakes were submerged as the boat heeled. I took notice when the floor boards began to float and bailed hard just to keep up with the water. With the bilge full, and the boat heeled, the water would wash up the inside of the hull splashing off the underside of the deck and out over the berths. It was a mess. We stopped at Glen Cove for the night, but even after we had tied up, I continued to bail for awhile until the bilge was empty. That was when I discovered the soft drink cans in the bilge that had popped open due to the boat's wild motion.

Thanks to experience I had worked out a better routine. When it's warm enough in the afternoon, I'll go for a swim. While in the water, I'll splash the hull sides then clean off any scum that's collected near the waterline. This is good exercise, and as long as I'm in the water, it's a good idea to bathe.

Some days, when it's hot and I'm feeling lazy, I'll flood the foot well in the cockpit with buckets of water just to keep cool. Or as boredom creeps in, I'll take the dinghy and scull around the anchorage just to talk with people. With the awning up over the Bear's cockpit you don't get much chance to stand up, so I would stand in the skiff when I sculled. Sooner or later, someone would request that I sing an Aria from an Italian opera, which, of course, I didn't know. "You must have the proper uniform," I would say with authority. Without my straw boater's hat and striped tee shirt I'm just not dressed for the occasion.

As the late afternoon moves into early evening, the social hour is at hand. Couples gather on various boats for cocktails when it begins to cool off. Sometimes I'm invited, which is always fun. And in turn, would extend an invitation to come and see the Bear. Few come, but those who do, tend to sit in their dinghies alongside. I think they consider her too small. One skipper even said, "It won't capsize if I come aboard will it?"

If no one drops by, my time is quietly spent observing the subtle changes of late afternoon as it transits into night. I watch as the blue sky slowly takes on a more golden tone as the sunset deepens.

Wildlife is most active at this time of day. Flocks of Red Wing Black Birds head west calling to each other, flying low overhead as the tall spars split the passing flocks. Swallows dart busily about the water's surface often joining in with bats to chase bugs. As the darkness deepens, only the bats remain, while the cadence of crickets increases accompanied by the deep bass of bull frogs.

As the cocktail parties finish aboard other boats, lights began to shine through cabin windows reflected on still waters as the sky continues to darken. I sit in the cockpit with an after dinner coffee. Those of us anchored out, like myself, have put up anchor lights, adding to the spectacle of reflected light, which in some small way, helps to fend off the coming darkness. As I continue to sit, sounds that carry easily across quiet waters are now limited to just a few voices and the occasional splash of an unseen fish.

There's a distinct chill in the air, tempting me to slip into the warmth of the cabin with its soft light playing on brass and varnish. For awhile, I amuse myself with the radio attempting to find new stations; before It's time to turn in. Meanwhile, the stars silently voyage through the night.

These are the quiet times that prove to be such good medicine for the restoration of the soul.

23 THE LONG BEAT HOME

Fall is in the air. The nights are noticeably cooler and the poison oak has been red on the levee banks for some time now. It's a constant reminder of the coming fall. Like the seasonal migratory birds, I have also become restless, feeling the urge to be on the move.

Sitting quietly in the cockpit, I watch the Bear hunt back and forth on her anchor in the light breeze before getting underway. There is little room for error in this crowded anchorage. The critical time starts the instant the anchor leaves the bottom. Securing the anchor quickly is critical as the Bear begins sailing with no one at the helm. During this time there can be trouble when other boats are anchored close at hand.

All goes well as the Bear struggles to overcome her leeway. Just as we are about to clear the closest boat to leeward, the wind shifts. Not having the speed to tack, we try to eke by on our existing momentum. The Bear clears the other boat's anchor line, but the skiff does not. It's dragged forward along the other boat's windward side and is certain to snag its anchor line. Quickly, I cast off the skiff. It blows back to leeward alongside of the anchored boat as the Bear circles downwind to catch the skiff. The timing is right. I grab the bow line of the skiff just before it reaches the tules. That gets some applause from several kibitzers watching from the boats across the way. "The luck of the Irish," I think as we sail into the clear.

After some short tacking out of Potato Slough, we are soon on the San Joaquin River and headed downwind toward Mandeville Cut. It is an open anchorage with lots of space just off the shipping channel. We pass Prisoners Point and the sheets are hauled in as we sail into Venice Reach. After sailing its length, we jibe over. Off in the distance are a few scattered boats at anchor. Most of the boats have bow lines to the shore with stern anchors out.

In the past I had anchored the schooner that way under sail just to see if it could be done. We managed, but it was quite tricky even with a crew in the cross current. I found it much easier to anchor out on the open water and swing in the breeze. As I learned from experience, not only was it cooler, but there were fewer bugs.

I spent a week or so at Mandeville exploring with the skiff and meeting friends before sailing farther up the San Joaquin. We anchored at Five Fingers which is very attractive, before turning back down the river again.

The decision to sail back down onto the bay hadn't really been made. At this point it had only materialized as a vague kind of restlessness, but nevertheless, we were drifting in that direction. No doubt, the fall color and cooler air had something to do with it. As the days continued to roll by, I began to feel the increasing weight of my obligations. The crowded anchorages had begun to thin out as yachts headed for the bay. However, at this point there were almost as many reasons to stay in the Delta as there were to head back.

Old Hutch kept slipping into my thoughts during this time of transition, even though I hadn't given him much thought in years. Burt

Hutchinson sailed a bear in the nineteen fifties and into the sixties before he was forced to give up sailing. He was a legend in the Delta. After being told it was impossible to sail his Bear in the delta, he decided to try it anyway. He told me the first year he took a crew just to be safe. After that he sailed alone.

Once he retired, his time in the Delta extended into the fall months, long enough to pick all the wild blackberries he needed for his preserves which he cooked onboard before sailing back down onto the bay. It was a smart move on his part.

In the fall we normally get good breezes from the northeast as the first of the storms offshore began to break through the summer's northwesterly wind pattern. Waiting for the right conditions, Hutch would sail back down onto the bay with the wind in his favor. As Hutch got older, someone donated an outboard motor intended for his Bear, but he used it on an old aluminum skiff instead. I had heard many stories about Hutch before ever meeting him. That's the way it is with legends.

When our courses finally did cross, I found him to be a delightful person full of stories about the Delta. The last time I saw Hutch was on Georgiana Slough. He was an honored guest aboard Blue Herron, a Herreshoff thirty ketch. Hutch at that time was no longer able to see well enough to sail. As I remember, one of Hutch's best stories was about knowing when to leave the Delta. "It always came to me in a dream," he said. "There I'd be, walking in downtown Stockton with no shoes on and wearing my old straw hat. That's when I knew it was time to go home."

The wind rushed through the rigging in a high pitched screech as we lay tied alongside a float at the Blue Heron Marina on Seven Mile Slough. It was blowing pretty good out there as I lay on my bunk listening with a book in my hand. Even though we had seen far more difficult conditions in the past, the wind still created a feeling of tension. I hoped the wind would quiet down, but it just wouldn't shut up. Moving to the navigation table, I reached for my tide book looking for answers, hoping to ease my wind-driven anxiety. However, that was not to be. The tides would be good for the next five days or so, with ebbs beginning in the morning. The last reason still holding me fast in the Delta had crumbled.

Perhaps it was just the restlessness of the wind that forced my decision, but clearly I knew it was time to go. We'd begin the sail home tomorrow even if it was blowing, but I hoped it would let off some just to make my life a little easier.

However, the following morning the wind was still at it. After a good breakfast the chart was laid out and the Bear was readied. She was side tied head to wind, but had very little space to leeward thanks to an old boat shed just under her lee. That could be a real danger in the high winds if the Bear's lee rigging should snag the shed's overhanging roof. After tying the skiff on a short line I was ready. The mainsail was up and luffing hard. Pushing the Bear forward, I ran hard down the dock until the Bear gained enough momentum to clear the shed before jumping aboard at the last moment. With the tiller and main sheet quickly in hand, I turned aft just in time to see the skiff smack the corner of the shed before we headed down Seven Mile Slough. It was a close call, but to my relief we were on our way.

Once out on the river, there was plenty of space to get the jib up and stow the halyard. It was wet work, so when finished I quickly retreated to the cockpit. The spray begin to rattle down on the dodger as I settled in keeping a close eye on the chart. A grounding could cost us hours and a lot of work before getting off. These sailing conditions were tougher than normal for the river. The wind blew hard against the outgoing tide. However, even at this point, it still wasn't any more difficult than sailing on San Francisco Bay.

As it was, the Bear took it all in stride. I was the one having difficulty. Navigation required that I tack every ten minutes or so just to stay in deep water. After what seemed like a long day, tack on tack, we finally arrived in Pittsburg by late afternoon.

Not feeling well, I took some aspirin. An early dinner was prepared and I hit the bunk. After twelve hours of sleep I felt better and was more than ready to take on the next leg of our sail home. Today we would cross Suisun Bay. Babe came to mind as he always did when beating down through Suisun Bay. Years ago he shared his knowledge with me.

Babe Fisher had spent decades in the Delta before I was born. As a boy, he remembered watching the scow schooners sail there. During World War Two he skippered a tug hauling barges on Suisun Bay. After the war, Babe hunted ducks in the bay's backwaters with friends and family. When I mentioned my difficulty sailing back through Suisun Bay, he pulled out the chart and showed how to follow the old scow schooner route. The scow schooners of the past didn't sail on the south side of Suisun Bay where the main channel is today, but cut behind Ryer Island, then came down the north side of the bay where the reserve fleet is now. This was a longer route in deeper water, but it provided a better angle of wind for sailing.

Even with Babe's help, I found Suisun Bay to be a formidable place. Someone told me that early Indians called Suisun, "The place of big wind."

The bay's water is mud brown with steep mean looking waves covering unmarked shoals that dry out during low tide. Partially surrounded by low lying islands and marsh its trees are terminally bent by the constant force of the wind. Most yachts that pass through these waters use the deep water channel on the south side and usually motor unless the wind is fair.

The local boats are mostly outboard fishing skiffs with small cabins, used to shelter their crews from the force of wind and spray. Almost no one sails here unless they have to.

The following morning we left Pittsburg Marina on New York Slough. This slough is pretty straightforward with fairly deep water close to its sides due to the shipping channel that runs through it. The weather was less than comfortable with overhead fog and a twenty-five knot wind blowing against the muddy ebb tide.

There used to be a tripod that marked the beginning of Middle Ground making it easier to find the cutoff to Ryer Island. The navigation aid blew down after decades of heavy winds.

After sailing a little past the now defunct old Middle Ground marker, I was forced to double back before finding the cutoff lost in the haze of the low lying backdrop behind Ryer Island. Once in the cutoff, our course became clear. The memories came flooding back of all the former boats that I had skippered through this cut, over to the reserve fleet, and then down the bay and into Carquinez Strait. We sailed through the cutoff in three easy tacks.

Next came the challenge of finding the buoy marking the entrance to Suisun Slough. Using the field glasses, the buoy was spotted as no more than a faint black dot. I've always used it as a guide through this narrow piece of water to avoid the unmarked Grizzly Bay shallows off to leeward and the Middle Ground shoals to windward.

After a half hour's sail, the day marks defining the reserve fleet which held a collection of forty or fifty mothballed ships came into view. From that point on the sailing was easier as we kept the pylons to port and stayed in deep water where we could shelter from the waves under the lee of the ships. After a few hours of beating to weather, we passed under the railroad bridge and entered Carquinez Strait on the last of the ebb.

It was a tiring sail, but the Bear handled it well. In fact, the Bear was the easiest of all the boats I've owned to sail back down onto the bay from the Delta. The wind vane did most of the work giving me the freedom to navigate and relax.

The Martinez Marina was just off to port so we ducked in for the night. The landing under sail was not difficult and this time we were given a berth near the the harbor entrance.

That night I went to a Mexican restaurant. The food was good and the place was crowded. It's just my guess, but because of my yellow float coat and sailing hat, it encouraged a young couple to share their table with me. As it turned out they had a Folkboat and they reminded me of when Sue and I were just starting to sail on the Bay.

When I mentioned the Mexican cruise, they asked why I didn't choose a Folkboat for the cruise. I told them Folkboats are a little larger and faster, but their masts aren't stayed as well, relying on single shrouds, nor are their hulls as strong without the built in strength of a bridge deck, or a self bailing cockpit needed for ocean sailing.

The following morning, before the sun came up, I was up and ready. Today's sail would be a long one. Sausalito, was almost thirty miles to windward. The trip would be even more difficult towing a skiff, especially when half that distance was sailed against the tide. So the sooner I was underway the better.

The wind was still blowing about the same as yesterday which would help to overcome the flood tide running against us. The ebb wouldn't start until just before noon.

Once the Bear was under sail, we headed over to the north side of Carquinez Strait looking for tide lines that would show any back eddies in our favor. Sailing in the shallow water would keep us from the worst of the current. An eagle eye was kept on the chart, and if there were any questions concerning depth, the sounding line was at the ready.

Sheltering from the current worked well until Dillon Point. There we were forced out into the full strength of the current as we struggled to clear the point. It took several hours more before we were able to pass under the Carquinez Bridge and sail by the Mare Island breakwater which juts out into San Pablo Bay. Tacking to starboard, we sailed for Point Pinole, which provided the most sheltered course with the last of the flood tide still running against us.

Once in San Pablo Bay, the wind vane did the sailing. As we passed Pinole Point the tide turned in our favor. Just as I dared to hope for better conditions and an easier sail, everything changed.

The wind shut down, leaving the Bear with slatting sails. The remaining waves made it impossible to use what little wind there was. The skiff was brought alongside and a towline was rigged. The sails were trimmed for beating with the tiller locked in place. I stepped into the skiff and began towing the Bear. Soon we were making headway with the sails full, thanks to my steady rowing. Occasionally the towline would temporarily go slack and the Bear would sail up on the skiff. I was pleased with our progress until the wind began to increase and the Bear overtook the skiff.

Now, rowing hard, I was alongside the Bear, but couldn't approach the boat because of the oars. As the Bear began to pass the skiff I quickly cast off the towline to avoid being dragged sideways and capsized.

The race was on!

Although the Bear wasn't moving very fast I continued to lose ground in the waves until the boat was several lengths ahead. The wind began to fade and I slowly gained on the Bear until finally coming alongside.

Then in one quick move, oars were stowed, and I grabbed the skiff's painter. I rolled aboard headlong into the cockpit in a most undignified manner.

Just as I was thinking I had made it, the weight of the skiff, dead in the water, yanked me up out of the cockpit leaving me stretched out across the stern deck until the skiff gained speed. This incident, of all things, was the most embarrassing of any. It reminded me so much of a scene from "The Russians Are Coming", when the town drunk chases the horse around the pasture so he can ride off to warn the town's people.

Several hours later, we were going well, popped out from under the Richmond San Rafael Bridge at the speed of a cork from a champagne bottle, thanks to the full force of the ebb. The sun was low in the western sky as we beat our way down Raccoon Strait before tacking into Richardson Bay.

The sail up the bay was like a second home coming. The wind had eased off considerably, leaving us to ghost through intermittent calms and minor gusts as we worked our way deeper into the bay. Finally the jib was dropped and we tacked up to the Cruising Club dock.

It had been a long day to say the least, and not one of my best considering what had happened in San Pablo Bay. It would be a long time before I would tow the Bear again with the skiff.

Completely exhausted and busy with putting a furl in the Bear's mainsail, I barely noticed through my fatigue that the club sat a little lower than usual. Something was odd, but I still didn't give it much thought as I focused on putting the boat to bed. Then while taking a breather, I did a double take, but still couldn't believe it. I had failed to notice that the yacht club had sunk.

Sunk!

Other members were in the club, wading around in their sea boots as though nothing unusual had happened. After putting my boots on, I climbed over the railing of the barge and waded into the club to find out what had happened.

The evening the club sank there was a party in progress when someone yelled, "Everyone off, the club is sinking!" Thanks to the determined progress made by wood boring Teredo worms, they had finally succeeded in torpedoing the club. The pumps could no longer handle the increasing inflow of water. Still in shock, I continued to mentally picture the club sinking when someone shouted the bar is open. This created a sudden stampede. Waves splashed against the bar, then rebounded across the room like a motorboat wake. Well, after all, it was a Saturday night!

As I waited for my drink a quiet toast came to mind. One of the club's usual suspects waded over remarking that he was surprised to see me. He asked how the cruise went and I gave him the short story, which was an abbreviated version of the truth. It made me think back to the suffering, hardship, and my struggle for survival with so much at stake. Those experiences, although not very pleasant at the time, had become the building blocks of personal courage and confidence. I began to think of this cruise as my legacy, not for fame or attention, but as the cornerstone for a start on a new life.

I believed I could do anything, but it was up to me to choose and be fully responsible for the consequences my actions. Deep inside, I instinctively knew what needed to be done. The rewards were there. It was just a matter of working smarter and sticking to the plan.

Silently, I raised my glass. "School starts on Monday. So here's to school, and the independence of a new single life!"

With that, I downed my drink, slammed the glass on the bar, and returned to the Bear.

DÉJÀ VU

As an old man, I struggle with illness, I stand in my garage and contemplate the passage of time between my first sail in the Bear and my last in the West Wight Potter, Ah Tiller the Fun.

As I think back over the years, I seldom spoke of the cruise, being ill at ease about its close calls, sharing only fragments of the story with friends. Those near disasters had a profound effect on me in several ways.

It was many years before the vivid dreams and flashbacks began to fade as I mentally re-played fighting to get back aboard the boat fifty miles offshore, or driving the Bear hard to windward in the middle of the night to escape the wild surf of a lee shore.

As the last of this story was being written, I came to see self-forgiveness as the answer for my past mistakes. It took 34 years to arrive at that conclusion. Over time I found myself driven to sail harder, faster, and better than my fellow sailors as compensation for those past errors made during the cruise. And no matter how much I won when racing, it was never enough to heal the regret of those past mistakes.

The damp coolness in the garage, brought on by the late afternoon fog, has chilled the air. It is time to return to the warmth of the house. Taking a moment, I pause to run my hand along the Potter's cockpit combing. She is dusty, neglected, and in need of sailing. I give her an affectionate pat.

I have come to the end of one curve. The dragon has been pulled from the cave and my conflicting emotions regarding the cruise have been resolved.

Now a new curve begins. The days are full of doctors' appointments and time spent in the hospital as I fight to defeat my illness. As I think back, this is not the first time I've been faced with a life and death struggle. The difficult memories of the cruise return, but this time to provide strength and endurance. Hopefully in the future, I will sail forth more gently, a wiser man, and much better for it.

ABOUT THE AUTHOR

Dave, do you want to put something here?

Insert author bio text here. Insert author bio text here

67400703R00089

Made in the USA
San Bernardino, CA
23 January 2018